412011

Changing Difference

D1609946

Changing Difference

———

The Feminine and the
Question of Philosophy

Catherine Malabou

Translated by Carolyn Shread

polity

First published in French as *Changer de différence* © Éditions
Galilée, 2009

This English edition © Polity Press, 2011

Polity Press
65 Bridge Street
Cambridge CB2 1UR, UK

Polity Press
350 Main Street
Malden, MA 02148, USA

ISBN-13: 978-0-7456-5108-8
ISBN-13: 978-0-7456-5109-5(pb)

A catalogue record for this book is available from the British Library.

Typeset in 12 on 14 pt Bembo
by Servis Filmsetting Ltd, Stockport, Cheshire
Printed and bound in Great Britain by MPG Books Group Limited,
Bodmin, Cornwall

The publisher has used its best endeavors to ensure that the URLs for
external websites referred to in this book are correct and active at the
time of going to press. However, the publisher has no responsibility
for the websites and can make no guarantee that a site will remain live
or that the content is or will remain appropriate.

Every effort has been made to trace all copyright holders, but if any
have been inadvertently overlooked, the publisher will be pleased to
include any necessary credits in any subsequent reprint or edition.

For further information on Polity, visit our website:
www.politybooks.com

Note

That "woman" finds herself now in the age of post-feminism deprived of her "essence" only confirms, paradoxically, a very ancient state of affairs: "woman" has never been able to define herself other than through the violence done to her. Violence alone confers her being – whether it is domestic and social violence or theoretical violence. The critique of "essentialism" (i.e. there is no specifically feminine essence) by gender theory and deconstruction is but one more twist in the ontological negation of the feminine.

Contrary to expectations, this ever more radical hollowing out of woman within movements of thought supposed to protect her, this assimilation of woman to a "nothing being" opens a new path. Let us then think this name "woman" as an empty but resistant essence, an essence that is resistant because empty, a resistance that strikes out the impossibility of its own disappearance once and for all. To ask what remains of woman after the sacrifice of her being is to signal, beyond both essentialism and anti-essentialism, a new era in the feminist struggle, changing the terms of the battle.

We begin here with philosophy, asking what, for a woman, is the life of a philosopher?

C. M.

Contents

Changing our difference:
that is translation

As I translated *Changing Difference: The Question of the Feminine in Philosophy* in the relatively safe space of Mount Holyoke, the first women's college in the United States, surrounded by a wider community that has a vibrant tradition of feminist activism and scholarship, I felt deeply Catherine Malabou's isolation, her acute awareness that the theoretical and institutional violence to which she is subject is but the 'civilized' lining of the brutality of most women's lives. My hope is that this translation will find many welcoming homes in English and an appreciation for Malabou's innovative attempt to bring together a renewed continental tradition in philosophy and the exciting rethinking that has emerged from gender and queer studies. Motivated by a refusal of the difference of the feminine as it is currently construed, Malabou's change starts with naming violence, but in looking for a change that does not only allay the patterns and power of violence but that changes change itself, she suggests a different tack.

In this book Malabou drops the pretence of the

detached, objective philosopher, just as I abandon the cloak of invisibility of the neutral translator. Without narcissism, she speaks to reiterate with all the other women who have insisted that they can speak, that yes, of course, the feminine does have a meaning and a sense, just as I add that the translator, too, speaks. And I say speaks – the translator, like the feminine, does not copy, does not mime; she speaks in the change that is translation, the change that aligns the practice of translation with Malabou's theorization of the plastic. Instead of perpetuating the argument against essence, against the power of the original text, with Malabou's changed difference, the translator makes peace with her profession, with her dedication to metamorphosis.

To change difference Malabou suggests we look beyond Hegel's resurrection of the phoenix, that we look beyond Derrida's web woven by the spider, to consider the regenerative powers of the salamander. I pick up her changes to bring them to a translation that really is well and truly over and done with that most "tedious old saying 'lost in translation'" (Luise von Flotow, *Translating Women*). This hole in the text, this gaping space of the feminine is not where meaning is swallowed, lost, or barred. No, this condensation precipitates the movement that is *tzimtzum*, the contraction and withdrawal that enables re-creation, the silence that allows for listening, the abbreviated edge where liberty is found.

Translator's preface

Just as philosophy contracts and drops ballast, so too translation sails on its own wind. We have neither to hold up the holy book, nor to burn it up entirely in a fit of violent despair; the space of the text is enough for plasticity, if only we can shift our fixed view of change as fixity unsettled. Starting with the wrinkle that will come to the text, we see the aging and renewal that is translation, the plastic possibility of translations that lie in every text. Translating *Changing Difference* invited me again to try to translate differently. To translate not by displacing, not by replacing, not by transferring. The challenge was to translate with the gesture of *tzimtzum*. Withdraw the French and make a hollow not of lost sense, but from a meaning for you, Malabou's readers in English.

Carolyn Shread

Introduction

There are two types of feminism today. Traditional feminism relies on the evidence of sexual difference, understood as the dualism of masculine and feminine. This feminism analyzes relations between the two sexes in terms of power and domination without ever questioning the presupposed dualism within the imperative of equality, parity, and reciprocity. Another, more recent, feminism, sometimes called "post-feminism," coming out of American gender studies and queer theory, challenges the binary division of the "genders." There are any number of possible sexual identities and the man–woman dualism is but a cultural construction. Examination of this construction reveals that the heterosexual matrix is not a natural given but rather an ideological norm whose function is to regulate and control behavior and identity codes.

Until now the putting into question of sexual difference and the shift from one feminism to the other have never been considered from a philosophical point of view. The idea of "gender" has never been taken back to its ontological source. Queer theory has never been confronted with deconstruction. The two intellectual traditions, American and Continental thought, have never been compared with each other. This book seeks to engage this dialogue.

Starting from my own experience as a "woman philosopher," I explore a new resistance by woman to the constant violence – theoretical and political – to which she is subjected all over the world every day. Beyond the dispute over "essentialism" and "anti-essentialism" (is there, or is there not, a "specificity" or "essence" of woman?) which has raged for years in post-feminism and which most of the time unleashes a pointless terrorism in what should be a debate, I seek recognition for a certain feminine space that seems impossible, yet is also very dangerous to try to deny. It may be that woman is only defined negatively with respect to the violence that is done to her and the attacks on her essence, but this negative definition nonetheless constitutes the resistant stock that distinguishes the feminine from all the other types of fragility, from overexposure to exploitation and brutality.

Of course, more than sexual difference itself, it is important to emphasize the differences that exist between women. I recognize that it is both abusive and unproductive to attempt to impose a single model on all the diverse political and social situations associated with the term "feminine." This is why I start from a concrete situation, my own, as a "woman philosopher," a French "woman philosopher." Here, in four interrelated texts, I explore the "meaning of the feminine" as well as the impossibility for woman to accede to philosophy without being immediately eclipsed as a subject.

All four of these texts, each in its own way, are addressed to Jacques Derrida, who accompanied me for so long and who was the first to show me the kind of difficulty that awaits a "woman" when she intends to become a "philosopher." Yet another difficulty was distancing myself from him, Jacques Derrida, in order to remain both: "woman" and "philosopher." As the last text shows, I had to do so in order to be neither "woman" nor "philosopher," through a decision that was none but my own and which was the pure, radical, and unconditional affirmation of my freedom.

It is freedom that is in question here, a freedom I throw on the page the way you fling a coat over your shoulder. A freedom dearly acquired, a freedom that required no less than for me to attempt to displace the concept of writing, to alter the trajectory of deconstruction, to plasticize *difference* and *différance*, in so far as I was able, of course, but in the most determined, obstinate, and solitary way possible. Today I might say that my fidelity to Derrida's thought is all the more precious because it was garnered through an open autonomy, whose complex birth is traced in the

3

two texts, "Grammatology and plasticity" and "The phoenix, the spider, and the salamander." As these two texts demonstrate, to speak of the feminine as a "philosopher" requires a revisiting of ontology and biology. The other two texts, "The meaning of the 'feminine'" and "Woman's possibility, philosophy's impossibility," measure the consequences of the first two in terms of sex and gender.

While it seemed more honest to me not to talk about "women in general" here, but to start instead from my own personal situation, my hope is that many women will follow the path outlined in this book and that the questions I ask – all of which concern a resistance of the feminine to its deconstruction – will resonate in each one in their own way, but with complicity and compassion.

I expect objections and even outright hostility. I confess, by the way, to not having much confidence in feminine solidarity, knowing all too well that there are just as many bitches out there as there are bastards. I write for them, too, anyway. But of course, first and foremost, I write for the women I love, the ones I do not know and who suffer mistreatment and humiliation. I write, too, for the women I know, the ones who, in their very way of being, carry with them something like an unlived memory of the others, a fragility that does not try to hide. I write for these women who, for this reason, are my friends.

The meaning of the "feminine"

> The two fleshy lips and two delicate folds of skin that surround the entrance to the vagina are called the "major" and "minor" labia (also known as "nymphs"). These folds form the rounded part of the vulva and present an elasticity, form, coloration, length, thickness and aptitude to become congested once excited, that is infinitely variable from one woman to another.
>
> *Le Robert, Dictionnaire de la langue française.*

If "woman" is understood as both a biologically and culturally determined reality, then we must acknowledge that the "feminine" no longer appears to be linked to "woman." The development of women's studies towards the end of the twentieth century, along with the work of Judith Butler in gender studies and queer theory, contributed to putting into question again the masculine/feminine divide and to showing that gender identity is always performative, never given. We now know that to speak of "genders" is no longer to speak of "sexes." Consequently we must

5

accept the idea that feminism can now be understood as a *féminisme sans femme*, a feminism without women. Woman as a predicate is no longer an obvious given, if in fact it ever was. So if the feminine has a "meaning," it is in as much as the permission to question the identity of woman follows from the deconstruction and displacement of this identity.

This situation also impacts the supposed integrity of the concept of "sexual difference," for to say that gender is constructed is to question difference understood as binary. There are not just two genders; there is a multiplicity of genders. Masculine and feminine can refer to several of these gender identities at once, without referring to originary anatomical or social givens.

It is now time to ask if there is any correlation between this pluralizing of gender differences and the pluralizing of ontological difference undertaken in France by a certain Heideggerian critical posterity. The concept of "ontological difference" is also found in the work of Levinas and particularly Derrida, where it is pluralized, delocalized, dislocated from its dual meaning. By reinterpreting difference as alterity and hospitality, Levinas opened the door of difference to a host of strangers to Being within Being; Derrida prolonged and radicalized this dissemination. In one as in the other, the idea of sexual difference played a determinant role in displacing the concept of ontological difference.

The meaning of the "feminine"

We must shed light on the link between a "cultural" and a post-Heideggerian ontological thought of gender, between American "critical theory" and the thinking of Being revisited by deconstruction, since this investigation has not yet been undertaken thoroughly. Can we say that there are ontological differences as one says that there are genders and that in both instances and in the same way, difference is more than duality?

This question, which points towards the possibility of a shared foundation for ontology and gender theory, immediately brings to mind two further questions. First, when we talk about gender difference and ontological difference, are we speaking about the "same" difference (in that it would be impossible to distinguish one from the other) or should we determine an order of priority or derivation? Second, if masculine and feminine have lost their traditional roles as sexual labels nowadays, opening out onto a plurality of possible identities, how do we explain that, at least among philosophers, the *feminine* enjoys a sort of ontological privilege over the masculine or transgender?

Clearly the "feminine" comes to be inscribed *between* the terms of the alternative opened by the first question about the simultaneity or derivation of the two types of difference, ontological and sexual. If, as Levinas claims, it is true that hospitality is the originary opening to the other, that is, to all differences and if it is true that the "feminine" designates not an individual identity but rather this opening or welcome itself, then there is not really any specificity or derivation of sexual difference in regard to ontological difference. The two come together, one for the other, and this play of reciprocity and simultaneity marks the place of the ethical. The ontic-ontological link could thus have the same meaning and speak the same language as the link between "feminine" and either "woman" or "man." "Woman" and "man" would thus have the same relation to the feminine, the same relation of source or origin as beings to Being.

But even if the feminine remains irreducible to any given gender, including the "woman" gender, it is still not a "neuter" word like Being. This is precisely why Levinas chooses it and endows it with ethical dignity. The feminine permits the "deneutering" of Being without bringing it back or reducing it again to the ontic register. To make Being and the feminine coincide is equivalent to "deneutralizing" *Dasein,* the being who is neither man nor woman and whose essence, Heidegger claims, precedes gender difference. The "masculine" could have played the same "deneutralizing" role, but, to answer the second question, by choosing the term "feminine," Levinas also sought to acknowledge a dimension of thought and ethics that had been excluded from Western metaphysics for all too long.

This point caused Derrida some difficulty. Although

in many ways he supported the move to deneutralize and feminize difference, he asked whether the feminine as thought by Levinas – as a welcome to all others – is really capable of resisting its reduction to this given being that is woman and whether it really could welcome other genders in its name.

In the ontological order, the question presents itself in the following terms: how far can there be a deneutralizing of Being that does not lead to a pure and simple metaphysical identification of being with Being? Can the feminine – and, again, why the feminine? – really be open, extending to all modes of Being? Isn't it always destined to characterize but one gender and to refer to but one type of being, namely "woman"? [1] At the same time, is any coincidence between being and Being metaphysical? Must we avoid this coincidence at all cost?

From the perspective of gender theory, the question presents itself in the following terms: must we really avoid the mark of sex in order to think gender? Is all sexualizing of gender outdated? Do beings and bodies benefit from being deneutralized, or should we think, on the contrary, that a certain transcendental disincarnation does harm to both the flesh and the concept of difference?

These questions always lead to a highly aporetic chain of reflection whose twists and turns I shall follow here – questions to questions – before finally pointing towards a new direction for reflection.

Changing Difference

Admiring the wonders of difference

Let us start with a "woman," Luce Irigaray, one of the only people to think explicitly together ontology and gender differences. Although Irigaray shares Levinas' position when she claims that there is no ethics that is not an "ethics of sexual difference,"[2] she displaces the ways of accessing this opening. Recognizing with Heidegger that all difference is first given as and through affect, that she *touches* before speaking, Irigaray adopts an affective tone that opens up to both Being and gender difference in a single movement – and this tone distinguishes her from Heidegger's "angst" or Levinas' "indolence" and "fatigue."[3] Irigaray's tone is *wonder* (in French *admiration*), understood in the sense that Descartes gives this term in *The Passions of the Soul*.[4] She writes, "To arrive at the constitution of an ethics of sexual difference, we must at least return to what is for Descartes the first passion: *wonder*. This passion has no opposite or contradiction and exists always as though for the first time."[5] To recall Descartes' definition:

> When the first encounter with some object surprises us and we judge it to be new, or very different from what we knew in the past or what we supposed it was going to be, this makes us wonder and be astonished at it. And since this can happen before we

know in the least whether this object is suitable to us or not, it seems to me that Wonder is the first of all the passions. It has no opposite, because if the object presented has nothing in it that surprises us, we are not in the least moved by it and regard it without passion.[6]

Wonder (*admiration*) should be understood in terms of the etymological meaning, which connects admiration to astonishment in the Latin verb "*mirari*." Wonder is the passion of surprise in the face of the extraordinary and the unfamiliar. Irigaray emphasizes its pre-predicative aspect: we wonder before judging. To wonder is to open oneself up to difference before granting it a value or establishing hierarchies. The anteriority of wonder to judgment prompts Descartes to call it the first of all passions. Wonder is the first of the six fundamental passions, preceding love, hatred, joy, sadness, and even desire. Later in her analysis Irigaray shows that wonder finds its necessary correlative in generosity, the ethical passion *par excellence* for Descartes, since it "causes us not to prefer ourselves to anyone."[7]

Wonder is the passion of difference; this difference is neither undetermined nor asexual. Irigaray's analyses push the Cartesian view further by viewing wonder precisely as the opening to gender difference. Even if we never wonder at anything other than difference and even if wonder is the ontological and

11

theoretical passion *par excellence* – Being is the wonder of all beings – in order for this difference to touch us, it must be inscribed within bodies since it is bodies that initially differentiate beings. The inscription of difference in bodies bears a certain mark, namely, gender. The other strikes us first through gender. Or rather, what is other in all others is gender, which is neither determined nor judged, since wonder suspends predication. Gender can only appear through its difference from another gender. Consequently, wonder, "the point of passage,"[8] allows the sexes to maintain a degree of autonomy grounded in their difference; it thus offers a space of freedom and desire, a possibility of separation or alliance. Considering the other with admiring wonder, in the Cartesian sense, it is impossible to assimilate them: in wonder, the other is "not yet assimilated or disassimilated as known," he or she is not absorbed, incorporated, or appropriated. "Wonder is a mourning for the self as an autarchic entity; whether this mourning is triumphant or melancholy. Wonder must be the advent or the event of the other. The beginning of a new story?"[9]

Genders cannot substitute for one another nor be assimilated to each other; they keep their secret. Since wonder does not have an opposite, it remains open, as an infinite difference that generosity extends: "Wonder constitutes an *opening* prior to and following that which surrounds, enlaces."[10] In this

non-reductive apprehension of the sexes, Irigaray
sees a way to clear an ethical space of recognition
of the feminine: the feminine as the affective union
between Being and sex(es).

The admiration of wonder is in fact structurally linked to the feminine in so far as it reveals the
ontological opening as a *maternity*. Because it is the
first of all passions, it is the *mother* of all desire. Thus
Descartes "situates woman in the place of the first and
last passion."[11] The mother-passion, the first woman
and last passion (last because it is the most complete,
the most accomplished), conditions all meetings
between genders, whether they are different or the
same. And so, because all subjects are able to wonder,
all subjects are feminine.

Why the "feminine"? Isn't the privilege of the feminine determined by the particular situation of "woman"?

An ethics of sexual difference has no need to determine the share of "man" and "woman" in the social
world, or to "define" the feminine; it need only see
in the feminine a space of between-genders, a space
of amazement and surprise that limits genders to
spaces without content, spaces that are empty and
hence inviolable. For Irigaray, the feminine does not
designate *a* gender, but rather the free play of genders,

their distance, their wonderful difference, the cusp of ethics once again.[12]

But we are still left with this word: "feminine." Why "feminine" if in the end it is no more attached to woman than to man? Why is the literalness of "feminine" still necessary? If this term does not designate *a* sex and can be expanded to transsexuality or to all of the occurrences of transgender, if it no longer refers exclusively to heterosexuality, if, through this reminder of the exclusion to which it is subjected, it can in a way also refer to other modes of being, other sexual practices, then why keep it? In the end, we have to admit that "feminine" does *owe* something to women!

This "debt" must be taken seriously. The choice of the feminine as the place of ethics is itself an ethical choice, which, as we know, seeks to put an end to the long tradition of exclusion and subordination of women and to their rejection from the ethical sphere, from thought, and from ontology. To elect the feminine is obviously to do justice to women, to transgress "phallogocentrism" through the promotion of what has always been trampled. But if we believe that the feminine cannot be understood without woman, then we also counter that "woman" cannot be understood without a certain determination which is that of her "sex." Yet another debt, another justice rendered: the choice of feminine recognizes precisely the *body* of woman, its morphology, the anatomy of her sex organs . . . So the link between the feminine, woman, and the woman's sex organs appears to be a reality that cannot be undone.

The vulva's schema

Isn't this contradictory? Didn't we just assert the independence of the feminine in regard to both anatomical and social givens?

In his work *On Touching – Jean-Luc Nancy*, Derrida sheds light on this problem. He acknowledges that Luce Irigaray cleared the way to a thought of the feminine through the updating of a certain type of affect, an affect of difference that appears to have escaped the metaphysics of auto-affection, which has determined the relation of the self to the subject in the philosophical tradition. But he recalls that, in some sense, the *morphology* of the woman *incarnates* this other mode of affection that is wonder, this touching without the predicative contact of the subject with him or herself. Why? Here Derrida refers to the passages where Irigaray thinks woman starting from a sort of self touching without self, without mastery or conscience, a space of withdrawal and separation without ego. This space is the space of the *lips*:

Since *Ce Sexe qui n'en est pas un*, Paris, Minuit, 1977 (*This Sex Which Is Not One*, trans. Catherine

Porter with Carolyn Burke [Ithaca, New York: Cornell University Press, 1985]), as we know, Luce Irigaray has been following and interpreting what is "at stake in woman's auto-eroticism" and the violence to which it is subjected when "The *one* of the form, of the individual, of the (male) sexual organ, of the proper name, of the proper meaning . . . supplants, while separating and dividing, that contact of *at least two* (lips) which keeps woman in contact with herself, but without any possibility of distinguishing what is touching from what is touched."[13]

Women's lips are as much those of her mouth as those of her vulva. But the vulva is better than the mouth at incarnating the existence of lips that cannot open by themselves, lips which, prior to penetration or expulsion (humors, blood, birth), are simply next to each other, split, Siamese, acritical. According to Derrida this priority of anatomy over ontology, this priority of the vulva (woman) over the concept (the feminine), is no contradiction. The lips of the vulva form a schema that places flesh *between* the sensible and the concept, without being one more than the other. Descartes' wonder also leaves us mouth agape, lips open-closed, suspending the ability to speak. The wonder-struck face becomes woman. There is no problem with this. Indeed, for Descartes a passion or an affect is unimaginable without the animal spirits, the blood, the parts of the body that support and materialize it.

Woman's lips are thus the logical, ontological, and physiological motif of an altering contact, the "self-touch you" (*"se toucher toi"*) of the subject affected by difference, to quote Jean-Luc Nancy's beautiful expression.[14] The lips suspend the opposition of me and other, activity and passivity: "it will never be known who/what is x, who/what is y in the female," writes Irigaray.[15] And, "Closed lips remain open. And their touching allows movement from inside to outside, from outside to in, with no fastening nor opening mouth to stop the exchange."[16] Furthermore,

> [. . .] The female sex. The threshold that gives access to the *mucous*. Beyond classical oppositions of love and hate, liquid and ice – a threshold that is always *half-open*. The threshold of the *lips*, which are strangers to dichotomy and oppositions. Gathered one against the other but without any possible suture, at least of a real kind. They do not absorb the world into or through themselves, provided they are not mis-used and reduced to a means of consumption. They offer a shape of welcome but do not assimilate, reduce, or swallow up. A sort of doorway to voluptuousness? They are not useful, except as that which designates a *place:* the very place of uselessness, at least as it is habitually understood. Strictly

speaking, they serve neither conception nor *jouis-sance*. Is this the mystery of feminine identity? Of its self-contemplation, of this very strange word of silence? . . . Both the threshold and reception of exchange, the sealed-up secret of wisdom, belief and faith in all truths?[17]

These fine analyses find a faithful echo in the frequent passages from Nancy found in *On Touching*, devoted to other lips, those of the mouth this time and not only the mouths "of women."[18] In this instance it concerns the difference in Latin between the mouth as *os, oris* and the mouth as *bucca*. The first, *os*, which also means face, is the mouth that speaks. The second, *bucca*, which is older than the first, is the mouth that eats, sucks, or feeds at the breast.

> The mouth that can scream, the closed mouth at the breast, thus opens up before the "oral stage." The mouth attaches itself to the breast in an "identification more ancient than any identification with a face," the "mouth slightly open, detaching itself from the breast, in a first smile, a first funny face, the future of which is thinking."[19]

This new distinction between lips and lips, between orality and buccality, proposed by Nancy, helps dissipate the apparent contradiction raised earlier regarding the link between the feminine and the vulva. The emphasis on the lips of the vulva would eventually be the opposite of a privilege. The lips of the woman's sex organ would become just one example, one among others, of the fact that lips do not have and never do have, one sole function; lips are always shared between several meanings. Regarding Nancy, Derrida writes, "The mouth *speaks* but it does so *among other things*."[20] In the same way, the lips of the vulva are lips *amongst others*. The lips of the sex organ, their type of contact have only a paradigmatic value in as much as they are one version of lips. The pluralizing of lips no longer stops with woman. Between the oral mouth and the buccal mouth, between the oral lips, buccal lips, and vulva's lips, between the "feminine" author (Irigaray) and the "masculine" author (Nancy), it is a question of openness and seniority, a morn more ancient than the dawn of metaphysics. This is why buccality in Nancy and the vulvar in Irigaray both lead us just as surely to the side of flesh as to the side of Being, to the opening of a mucous membrane as to the ontological opening.[21] The specificity of the feminine anatomic sex organ is both affirmed and erased in the "among others" of the mouth.

Without necessarily saying a word, all these mouths speak of the existence of a "hetero-affection," from one touching to the other, from one touch of difference that haunts and displaces right from the start touching understood as the testing of the

19

subject's self-presence. Now, the different mouths of hetero-affection delocalize woman's privilege but nevertheless characterize this origin as being the "feminine" itself. The open, the morn, the mucous, all relate to the breast. In the light of these developments, it is no longer clear what might prevent us from understanding hetero-affection starting with the feminine and the feminine itself starting with a certain non-reflexive structure of lips.

Isn't the meaning of the feminine hetero-affection? On the other hand, can hetero-affection have any other meaning than the one it has in and as the feminine? How could hetero-affection transcend the feminine, how could it not stop there?

The dangers of deneutralizing difference, or the ambivalence of the feminine

Derrida firmly resists this coincidence. Even if he comes very close to understanding hetero-affection as the meaning of the feminine, even if, truth to tell, we are never far from an interpretation of the openness to difference as the interpellation of gender difference, for Derrida there is an irreducible gap between all these terms. Ontological difference and gender difference, hetero-affection and the feminine sit resolutely side by side without confusion. There is a slip, a discontinuity, a *"faux-bond"*[22] between them and this is the danger of a triple reduction caused by their possible coincidence: the reduction of difference or alterity to the feminine; the reduction of the feminine to woman; and, lastly, for Derrida, the reduction of hetero-affection to auto-affection is never totally dispelled.

Derrida's *Adieu – to Emmanuel Levinas*[23] is no doubt the text that exposes this tripartite danger the most clearly through a divided reading. On the one hand, Derrida acknowledges that for Levinas the feminine is not necessarily linked to a particular being who is "woman." On the other hand, he shows that for the author of *Totality and Infinity* the feminine appears to refer purely and simply to "the femininity of 'Woman.'"[24] "Woman," in this second instance, would not be an anatomic-ontological mode of being of the lips but rather, trivially, "the companion of man." "Need one choose here between two incompatible readings?" asks Derrida.[25] That is precisely the question.

Let us start by detailing the two possible readings of Levinas. In describing the first reading, Derrida reminds us that for Levinas there is no gap between the "Other" and the "feminine." They can be thought of as synonymous, as exhausting each other. Femininity is not a specific mode of hospitality, but rather hospitality itself. This is its "ontological" meaning which ensures that the feminine is not restricted to woman. This passage in *Totality and Infinity* states it clearly:

The home that founds possession is not a possession in the same sense as the movable goods it can collect and keep. It is possessed because it already and henceforth is hospitable for its proprietor. This refers us to its essential interiority and to the inhabitant that inhabits it before every inhabitant, the welcoming one par excellence, welcome itself – the feminine being.[26]

Derrida comments:

The absolute, absolutely originary welcome, indeed, the pre-original welcome, the welcoming par excellence, is feminine; it takes place in a place that cannot be appropriated, in an open "interiority" whose hospitality the master or owner receives before himself then wishing to give it.[27]

The feminine element of the dwelling does not assume the *de facto* existence of woman: there is no need for a woman in the house to apprehend the feminine as another name for hospitality. Levinas states this emphatically:

Need one add that there is no question here of defying ridicule by maintaining the empirical truth or countertruth that every home *in fact* presupposes a woman? The feminine has been encountered in this analysis as one of the cardinal points of the horizon in which the inner life takes place – and the empirical absence of the human being of "feminine sex" in a dwelling nowise affects the dimension of femininity which remains open there, as the very welcome of the dwelling.[28]

And so in many ways the feminine is not reducible to woman. When Levinas thinks the feminine as intimacy, doesn't he think of it as a form of withdrawal similar to the "fold" of lips? When he writes that "woman is the condition for recollection," "the separation that is concretized through the intimacy of the dwelling,"[29] doesn't he warn us against the violence involved in forcefully opening these lips? Don't Levinas and Irigaray agree that the lips of the feminine, the feminine of lips, irreducible to any gender, are the carnal version of a moment that could be called transcendental, without giving priority to either? An instance that reveals the fragility, the defenseless withdrawal, which thereby implies, through its reversal, the possibility of evil as rape.[30]

Perhaps more than any other schema the silent, withdrawn and folded lips, offered and defenseless, of the woman's anatomical sex organ allow us to figure absolute, defenseless fragility. But this schema does not also play the role of model or paradigm. Nothing prevents us from seeing the two lips in other beings than woman, seeing them in any exposed, suffering subject. Nor must we forget that defilement, rape,

and evil can also be the acts of women. The violence
done to lips can come from everywhere; it can be the
fact of anyone, the work of all, including women. As
Judith Butler says, it is necessary to think of the possibility of a feminine penetration, or more precisely, a
penetration of the feminine by a woman, either good
or bad.[31] Obviously woman can desecrate the feminine, perpetrate evil, abuse children, other women,
men, animals, or offend justice and thought . . . The
feminine is detachable from "woman."

Let us turn now to the second reading. In this light
we see that some very fine analyses of the feminine as
ontological given also convey archaic and conserva-
tive views of the role of women. In the end, even
given the precautions taken by Levinas, it appears to
be difficult to separate the ethical interiority of the
feminine from a pragmatic view of domestic woman.
In *Totality and Infinity* we read of a woman who serves
man silently: "Those silent comings and goings of the
feminine being whose footsteps reverberate the secret
depths of being are not the turbid mystery of the
animal and feline presence whose strange ambiguity
Baudelaire likes to evoke."[32] The motifs of welcome
and hospitality also serve to put femininity back in
her place: domesticity, the eternal essence of woman.

This strange "space" of woman as the "being in
the dwelling" is confirmed in the text entitled "And
God Created Woman." Levinas proposes an exegesis
of the passage from Genesis (2, 22): "And the Lord

The meaning of the "feminine"

God fashioned into a woman the rib he had taken from man." The commentary is ambiguous. On the one hand, there is no primacy or priority of man over woman:

> The meaning of the feminine will thus become clear against the background of a human essence, the *Isha* from the *Ish*. The feminine does not derive from the masculine; rather, the division into feminine and masculine – the dichotomy – derives from what is human.[33]

On the other hand, Levinas returns to a commentary of the Talmud on the same topic:

> Here is the response of Rav Abbahu: God wanted to create two beings, male and female, but he created in God's image a single being. He created less well than his original idea. [. . .] He wanted two beings. In fact, he wanted that from the beginning there should be equality in the creature, no woman issuing from man, no woman who came after man. From the beginning he wanted two separate and equal beings. But that was impossible; this initial independence of two equal beings would no doubt have meant war. [. . .] To create a world, he had to subordinate them one to the other. There had to be a difference which did not affect equity: a sexual difference and, hence, a certain preeminence of man, a woman coming

later and as woman and appendage of the human. We now understand the lesson in this. Humanity is not thinkable on the basis of two entirely different principles. There had to have been a *sameness* that these *others* had in common. Woman was set apart from man but she came after him: *the very femininity of woman is in this initial "after the event."*[34]

So even if the feminine is the origin of ethics, this primacy is nonetheless an afterthought. It seems that Levinas does not really distinguish the ontological primacy of the feminine from the seconding of woman, her condition as "the companion of man," coming *after* him.[35] The ethical privilege of the feminine is accompanied here strangely by the social secondariness of woman. And the conclusion is clear as day: "You see: the feminine is in a fairly good position in this hierarchy of values [. . .]. It is in second place."[36]

Clearly we are faced with the possibility of two incompatible readings. On the one hand we have what Derrida calls "a sort of feminist manifesto," since Levinas goes so far as to "confer the opening of the welcome upon '*the feminine being*' and not upon the *fact* of empirical women." In this light, the feminine would be the name of the "pre-ethical origin of ethics."[37] Yet, on the other hand, we recognize, "so as then to question [. . .] the traditional and androcentric attribution of certain characteristics to woman (private interiority, apolitical domesticity, intimacy of a sociality that Levinas refers to as a 'society without language,' etc.)."[38] Aren't the freedom of the feminine, the proliferation of genders brought back to the dyad? Isn't ontological difference forgotten once again in favor of a "sexual difference" which soon reduces difference to duality?

The same ambiguity is found in Irigaray's work, which does not always avoid this tying back in of the feminine to woman and the rigid and simplistic binary of the masculine and the feminine. In her work it is a matter of contesting the secondariness of woman, but in the end the problem is the same as in Levinas. Indeed, the "feminist" discourse which tends to oppose the feminine – understood as femininity *of woman* – to masculine domination, simultaneously restricts the meaning of the feminine understood as openness and plurality. Once again binaries dominate, along with their strict and often uncritical definitions. Thus in Irigaray the play of the lips touching, analyzed above, is sometimes simply thought in its difference (in the sense of a simple, rather than ontological distinction) from the "'to touch oneself,' of the masculine gender, is defined as that which begins to set up the distinction subject–predicate, subject–object."[39] Here again there are two possible readings. Irigaray certainly does not always harden the distinction between masculine and feminine, and, as we have seen, wonder gives access to a difference without opposition, to this empty and multiple space of between-genders, within which there is not any real conflict between a feminine and a masculine self-touching. At other times, however, difference appears very clearly as an *ontic* confrontation between the feminine and the masculine, where the "feminine" signifies the exclusion of woman within the irreducible asymmetry of genders in tradition. In this dissenting framework the "lips" mark (and now mark only) the possibility of a "properly" feminine sexuality in contrast to the all-powerful phallus. Once again the proliferation of gender appears to be lost.

Judith Butler offers a critique of this problem in *Gender Trouble*:

> The return to biology as the ground of a specific feminine sexuality or meaning seems to defeat the feminist premise that biology is not destiny. But whether feminine sexuality is articulated here through a discourse of biology for purely strategic reasons, or whether it is, in fact, a feminist return to biological essentialism, the characterization of female sexuality as radically distinct from a phallic organization of sexuality remains problematic. Women who fail either to recognize that sexuality as their own or understand their sexuality as partially constructed within the terms of the phallic economy are potentially written off within

the terms of that theory as "male-identified" or "unenlightened."[40]

If we reduce "the feminine" to woman and lips to "feminine" sexuality, then we produce the very exclusion we were trying to avoid. From "anatomical-ontological difference" to "biological essentialism," the lips or vulva then change their meaning, turning back against themselves, that is, against the "feminine."

The reason for this ambivalence in Levinas and Irigaray's positions perhaps derives from the fact that identifying one instance as "the feminine," in the ontological and ethical sense first proposed, always leads thought to rigidify something under this name as an essence. Indeed, isn't the "feminine" always condemned ultimately to stand as a structural and ahistorical paradigm superseded or exceeded by a historical reality that is always moving, namely gender? Perhaps naming the space of play of genders "feminine" amounts to blocking the game itself. Judith Butler, who refuses to give "a" "meaning" to the "feminine," asks the following question: "Is it possible to identify a monolithic as well as a mono-logic masculinist economy [of the feminine] that traverses the array of cultural and historical contexts in which sexual difference takes place?" She continues further, "Is the failure to acknowledge the specific cultural operations of gender oppression itself a kind of epistemological imperialism?"[41] Clearly the "feminine" is touched here in its double structure: ontological ("monolithic as well as a monologic masculinist economy" referred to in its very name) and ontic (the "feminist" opposition of "feminine" to "masculine"). In both instances, the plural eludes difference. And this is where we come back to Derrida: even when it believes it is opposing it, the ontic-ontological imperialism of the feminine does nothing but repeat the metaphysics and phallocentrism that we know are one and the same.

To come finally to the danger of the third reduction, the reduction of hetero-affection to auto-affection, it is clear to Derrida that the Cartesian theory of the passions can only serve the ambiguity analyzed earlier. Even if there is definitely no way to "choose between two incompatible readings, between an androcentric hyperbole and a feminist one" opened by the texts on the feminine, even if there is no "place for such a choice in ethics,"[42] even if we cannot choose between Levinas and Levinas, Irigaray and Irigaray, the feminine and woman, their ambivalence remains. Thus the Cartesian thought of alterity as infinity within the self, reinterpreted by Levinas, is still a type of reduction of the other to the same for Derrida, since it involves the violence done to the other by containing it within the subject. Wonder is nothing but a variation of this violence. For Derrida this is precisely the difficulty contained in the concept of "*Stimmung*" or "affective tone" (attunement) in general, as in any affect of difference (not just the affects privileged by Heidegger, but any type of affect as well): *Stimmung* is always linked to a kind of interiority, the interiority of *Dasein* alone, who auto-affects, that is, temporalizes the self. And in the end how can we believe that Cartesian wonder and generosity can be anything other than the affects of identity?

In *On Touching* Derrida claims that ultimately Descartes' generosity always remains "the virtue of a subject."[43] This generosity must be distinguished from another one, which is no longer the generosity of a subject but well and truly a "generosity of Being," an originary gift.[44] This generosity would be "a generosity of *ethos* more than an ethic of generosity."[45] The reversal is important, since it suggests that ethics cannot be identity-based, that it is necessary to imagine a generosity or wonder that is not limited to any given being. Perhaps to "deneutralize" difference, to think it from the feminine, would always amount to limiting it, to restricting the primordial opening of the originary welcome or gift.

This is why Derrida never offers any "meaning" of the "feminine." The feminine is there, written everywhere in his work, but it slips like an eel, without any specific home or privilege. It keeps at a respectful distance from Being, from difference, from the sexes, and from gender.

The neuter and evil

To speak of the "feminine" would thus lead, one way or another, to a reinforcement of traditional divisions and a reduction in the breadth of difference. However, and this is the point I now wish to analyze, the critique of feminine specificity also leads to a dead end.

It is surprising to note that, despite the radical upheaval he brings to Heideggerian thought, Derrida does not really touch on the neuter or the neutrality of *Dasein* as thought by Heidegger. The neuter can be troubled, it can be discussed, but contrary to all expectations it remains, in some senses, undeconstructible. In the article "Sexual Difference, Ontological Difference," Derrida claims that despite what one might first imagine, the neutrality of *Dasein* described by Heidegger corresponds less to a neutralization of sex life than to a neutralization of the binarism or duality of the sexes supposed to constitute the possibilities of this life. Heidegger would in fact open up

> thinking to a sexual difference that would not be [. . .] sexual duality, difference as dual. As we have already observed, what [Heidegger] neutralized was less sexuality itself than the "generic" mark of sexual difference, belonging to one of the two sexes. Hence, in leading back to dispersion and multipli-

cation [. . .], may one not begin to think a sexual difference [. . .] not sealed by a two? [. . .] The withdrawal of the dyad leads toward another sexual difference.[46]

There are "sexual *differences.*"[47]

If sexual difference is thus pluralized ontologically, there is no more reason to elect the feminine to the rank of the instance of ethical openness, the welcome to the other and the origin of wonder, availability to difference, or to the space of play between the genders. Just like any other gender identifier, the feminine becomes "a free floating artifice,"[48] to borrow Judith Butler's expression. From the proliferation of genders, one might now say that the feminine is consistent but non-existent, that the feminine consists without being, that is without being a being.

Yet we know that Levinas does not like the phrase, "without being a being." Levinas does not believe in hunting down the ontic. Even when ontological difference is recognized, especially when it is acknowledged and taken seriously, we are never dealing with mere Being. We recall the preface to the second edition of *Existence and Existents*, which calls for a deneutralization of ontological difference for the sake of paying attention to beingness. Being(s), or the existent, makes difference legible. This legibility, written on us like an ethical injunction, is the other name of the feminine. From that point, admittedly, alterity is an existent and the feminine can no longer be thought without women existents. And what's wrong with that? While of course one must avoid reifying the Other, one must also, inversely, avoid disincarnating, that is, de-beingifying Others.

After all, once again, where's the harm in linking alterity to a being, the feminine, and sometimes linking the feminine to woman? Where's the harm, since for Levinas the feminine refers precisely to fragility, to the exposure to evil, which cannot be separated from a certain schematic role of woman – and here we come back to Irigaray – the schema of the fold of the lips to one another, a withdrawal that is so easy to force open, to breach, to deflower, but which at the same time also marks the territory of the inviolable? In the final instance the meaning of the feminine is just that: the inviolable. Without the feminine, the inviolable cannot be thought. The neuter would already be profanation.

Derrida understands this perfectly and declares,

> Never will any contact breach the virginity of this femininity of the *Aimée*, the feminine Beloved (Levinas never, I think, speaks of the *Aimé*, the masculine Beloved). One can indeed violate her but only to run aground before her inviolability. [. . .] Femininity is only violable, that is, like the secret that it is, inviolable. "Feminine" signifies the locus

------

of this "contradiction" of "formal logic": violable inviolable, touchable untouchable.[49]

But, still not convinced by this answer, you ask, why the feminine? Isn't the inviolable figured everywhere, without any privileged schema, by innocence wherever it is offered, in the fragility of the child, the stranger, the victim, or the animal? As Derrida says, "There is an implacable configuration there: femininity, infancy, animality, irresponsibility."[50] The inviolable is not *one* life, but the living of life, the minimum suffering, the treasure of nakedness, vulnerability, immunity. So then why, even if the lips of the woman's sex organ are one of the least disappointing hypotyposes,[51] that is, the closest to fragility, why call this live treasure "feminine"? Why risk defining this anonymity, in other words, the neutrality of fragility, which is equitable and just precisely because it does not have an exemplary being?

But, to return to the aporia, one might also ask why not? Should we and must we do otherwise? This is a difficult question to answer. If we name it the feminine, if we incorporate the inviolable, we do run the risk of fixing this fragility, assigning it a residence and making a fetish out of it. If we resist it, we refuse to embody the inviolable and it becomes anything at all under the pretext of referring to anyone. To do so is to interrupt a void in difference. Not to do so is to refuse to interrupt a void in difference. In the end, from an ethical perspective, both are equally justifiable, which is to say, they remain unjustifiable.

While you can see, you can also not see, why it would be more feminist to say that the feminine is not necessarily and factually linked to woman than to claim that empirical femininity cannot be erased and is resistant to any neutralizing roller. What is feminism if it involves eradicating its origin, woman? On the other hand, if it is true, if the feminine is defined with reference to the being who "remains in the home" or the one who does not have the phallus, then the pre-ethical origin of ethics will always be suspect . . .

In the end, I believe that the ontological question must be displaced. At the beginning I recalled that Levinas and Derrida definitively pluralized ontological difference. Beings form many different figures and the question of alterity digs out space for an infinite number of arrivals in the flesh of difference. However, despite this, the mode of relation of Being and being has itself never been rethought. The gap is still its only mode of being.

Yet ontological difference means nothing (even if it is written in the plural as ontological difference*s*) if one does not recognize that the gap is doubled by substitutability. Being and being change from one into the other; as I tried to show in *The Heidegger Change*,[52] that's the plasticity of difference. Being and being are different but they exchange modes of being. There is no gap without exchange or reciprocal metamorphosis. If Being is thought of as a being in the metaphysical tradition, that is because it offers itself as a being and this play continues, *very differently but according to the same rule of substitutability, beyond metaphysics.*

If this is true, then we must once and for all stop seeing this exchange as a specificity or "incarnation," in the metaphysical sense, of Being. Substitutability is the meaning of Being. Transvestitism comes with difference. It is taken in the "Fold." To interrogate the ontological meaning of gender theory necessarily amounts to elucidating the relation of difference to transvestitism, that is, to change. For Heidegger,

> There is, at departure, a rush of presence to the door of exchange, a rush that is nothing if not a metamorphic and migratory influx. Prior to exchange, nothing. Everything goes at the outset into the converter. And so it begins: difference. Heidegger shows that this first offer – metaphysics is what makes Being a first offer – is something irreducibly older than self-exposure in prostitution, self- (ex-) change in alienation, disguise, mendacity, or imposture. [. . .] which means that from the dawn of the West, whoever announces himself by declaring "I am" has always in reality been saying, "I am originally changed [changé]."[53]

Originally exchanged.

———

Being cannot be thought without its ontic transformability and we must now start to pay attention
to this plastic structure if we hope to bring down
the wall that Heidegger's critical posterity built up
between Being and being. The difference of Being
and the being in no way prevents us from imagining their exchangeability. We know *one* mode of
this substitutability (and often that's all we know):
metaphysics itself, in which being takes the place
of Being. But the "other thought," born of the
end of metaphysics, certainly does not seek to
conclude substitution in general, it announces an
other substitutability of Being and the being, understood as the *free circulation* of both, *play*, exchange
structure without domination or appropriation of
one by the other. From then on, the transvestitism of Being as the being and the being as Being
takes on an entirely different meaning: they point
at one another, show one another to each other,
lose their identity even as they gain it in this
game of the unfamiliar, the strange, the queer.
So long as we think ontological difference outside
the transvestitism to which it necessarily gives rise,
including and above all metaphysics, no theory of
the pluralization of difference will be able to shake
the rigidity of the dyad. So long as the being is
thought of as derived and secondary in relation to
Being we will not be able to understand the new
ontological transformability Heidegger announces

from the time of *Contributions to Philosophy*. It is clear that for him, *the forgetting of beings* has always doubled the *forgetting of Being*. To think through this forgetting is to give the dynamism of its power of exchange back to difference. Difference is a trader, not a principle for selection or for dual segregation.

As one of my former students at Berkeley, translator Peter Skafish, wrote to me, according to this new ontological reading which assumes "*the going-in drag of* essence," there is no reason to privilege the "feminine," or to name the crossroads of ontic-ontological exchange "feminine." If it is true that its structural potential for exchange is part and parcel of the meaning of being, then the feminine is both one of the possible modes of this meaning or one of the ontic substitutes of being in the exchange process. This point brings us back to the shared etymological origin of *genus* and *gender*: *genos*, genre as essence. If this essence is thought of as "changing," if transformability defines its ontological status, the problem is no longer that the "feminine" can be "reduced" to woman (once again, I find the cautions against this sort of "reduction" just as suspect as the supposed reduction itself). The question is that while the feminine or woman (we can use the terms interchangeably now), remains one of the unavoidable modes of ontological change, they themselves become passing, metabolic points of identity, which like others show the passing inscribed at the heart of gender.

Once and for all then, the potential for exchange that lies at the heart of ontological difference must also come out of the closet.

Grammatology and plasticity[1]

In *Of Grammatology* Jacques Derrida argues that until now there has never been a true "science of writing." The term "grammatology," defined as "a treatise upon Letters, upon the alphabet, syllabation, reading, and writing,"[2] has only ever been used to classify histories concerned with the appearance, genesis, and transformations of writing, leaving the status of writing as concept and scientific object in the shadows. In so far as writing has always been considered an auxiliary to speech, a derivative of speech lacking all autonomy, it has never elicited more than a few chapters or even pages in linguistic treatises. There is not a single "Course in general grammatology" and grammatology has never been designated the "project of a modern science."[3]

Of Grammatology proposes to develop and implement just such a project. Derrida's intention is to lay the foundations for a veritable science: "the concept of writing should define the field of a science."[4] This is stated explicitly in the title of the third chapter, "Of grammatology as a positive science," in which

Derrida claims that "the constitution of a science or a philosophy of writing is a [. . .] difficult" but "necessary task."[5]

The question I now wish to ask is as follows: why has this grammatological project never come to fruition? Why, despite Derrida's statements, has a scientific "grammatology" never seen the light of day? Why has the "science of writing," in the new sense it is given, never been established? Why does the title *Of Grammatology* refer only to a book, rather than to a treatise universal in scope, capable of engendering a scientific posterity in the same way as linguistics, for example?

There are two types of reason for this "failure." First, there are the reasons Derrida advances. In his 1992 lecture, "For the Love of Lacan," he referred back to the 1967 text, saying,

> *Of Grammatology* was first the title of an article [. . .] and – this is one of the numerous mistakes or misrecognitions made by Lacan and so many others – it never proposed a grammatology, some positive science or discipline bearing that name; on the contrary [. . . it] went to great lengths to demonstrate the impossibility, the absurdity, in principle, of any science or any philosophy bearing the name "grammatology." The book that treated *of grammatology* was anything but a grammatology.[6]

Grammatology and plasticity

These statements show clearly that the "failure" of grammatology was programmed . . . by grammatology itself. The Derridean redefinition of writing is the foundation of grammatology even as it denies the very concept of science. We must therefore acknowledge that the conditions of possibility of grammatology are precisely the causes of its impossibility.

But perhaps there is also a second reason for this "failure," one which derives less from the aporetic nature of the deconstruction of the traditional concept of writing – the deconstruction that prohibits any positive theory or philosophy of writing – than from an area of shadow lurking in deconstruction itself, and therefore also shading the redefinition of writing it proposes. I wish to focus on this darkness that negatively reveals writing's "plasticity" – to introduce a new term that I'll explain in the course of this analysis.

Let's start by going back to the opening pages of *Of Grammatology*. In a critical discussion of Saussure's semiology project, the need for a modern science of writing is quite clear. In chapter 2, "Linguistics and grammatology," Derrida argues that we must substitute a "grammatology" for the "general semiology" whose epistemological outline Saussure presented in his *Course in General Linguistics*:

A science that studies the life of signs within society is conceivable; it would be a part of social psychology

43

and consequently of general psychology; I shall call it *semiology* (from Greek *sēmeîon*, "sign"). Semiology would show what constitutes signs, what laws govern them. [. . .] Linguistics is only a part of the general science of semiology; the laws discovered by semiology will be applicable to linguistics and the latter will circumscribe a well-defined area within the mass of anthropological facts.[7]

Derrida comments that the difficulty lies in the impossibility for semiology to free itself from linguistics in order to go beyond the limitations it imposes. Contrary to Saussure's claims, Derrida points out that linguistics could never become merely "part" of semiology. Indeed, the concept of the sign at work in the determination of the meaning of the term "semiology" is itself governed entirely by its linguistic understanding,[8] thereby remaining dependent on a conception of language that sees in it a whole stratified into derivations within which the written sign comes after speech and is limited to being no more than the "signifier of the signifier."[9]

A grammatology becomes necessary when the thought and knowledge of language demand to be freed from linguistics. Only a grammatology can make "linguistics-phonology" a merely "dependent and circumscribed" area of a science of signification.[10] Why? Because grammatology is in some senses a semiology without signs. So long as thought is situated within the strict limits of a logic of signs, it will remain prisoner to a phonetic and phono-logic determination of language in which writing is always secondary. So long as we continue to speak of signs, including the written sign, knowledge remains tributary to an understanding of the signifying referral attached to the model of the natural relation between voice, mind, and meaning.

This relation presupposes a "natural bond of the signified (concept or sense) to the phonetic signi-fier," a natural link between "the *phonè*, the *glossa*, and the *logos*."[11] Yet the idea of this "natural" link contradicts what Saussure terms the arbitrariness of the sign. Originally, signification is immotivated and grammatology alone can claim to be a science of immotivation:

> Science of "the arbitrariness of the sign," science of the immotivation of the trace, science of writing before speech and in speech, grammatology would thus cover a vast field within which linguistics would [. . .] delineate its own area [. . .]. By a substitu-tion which would be anything but verbal, one may replace *semiology* by *grammatology* in the program of the *Course in General Linguistics*.[12]

However, as I said earlier, we have to admit that this type of grammatology has never "entered upon the assured path of a science." Never has grammatology constituted itself as a "discipline" in Derrida's oeuvre, either individually or generally, for it has never become an area of knowledge in its own right. In fact, in Derrida's writing the grammatological project goes no further than *Of Grammatology*. It never comes up again either in contemporary texts such as *Writing and Difference*, or in later texts.

There is not, never was, and certainly never will be a general semiology, but nor is there, was there, or ever will there be a general grammatology either. Derrida doesn't even use the word grammatology except to refer to the 1967 text. So why did grammatology disappear no sooner had it appeared?

Derrida himself offers several reasons. From the very first pages of the book he states that "such a science of writing runs the risk of never being established as such and with that name. Of never being able to define the unity of its project or its object. Of not being able either to write its discourse on method or to describe the limits of its field."[13] Indeed, as we know, *Of Grammatology* notes the limitations of the classic *epistemè* while simultaneously claiming a certain closure of knowledge. Thus there cannot be a real *science* of writing. "Graphematics or grammatography ought no longer to be presented as sciences; their goal should be exorbitant when compared to grammatological knowledge."[14] Grammatology can no longer be considered a human science: "What seems to announce itself now is, on the one hand, that grammatology must not be one of the *human sciences* and, on the other hand, that it must not be just one *regional science* among others."[15] Grammatology cannot be a science like any other.

But this answer is not really satisfactory. It obviously contradicts the clearly stated goals of the work: *despite everything else*, grammatology is well and truly presented as a science, as a program, as the necessary suite to linguistics, the successor to general semiology. What, then, are we to make of the peculiar fate of the "science" of writing?

To further the analysis of these questions, we must examine that which is often considered as (too) well known, namely the upheaval to which Derrida subjects the traditional concept of writing.

The meaning of the word "grammatology" can only change, can only cease referring to the history of writing and become the name of a real science of writing if it is grounded in a deep change in the meaning of the concept of writing itself. "Writing" can no longer simply refer to the technique of noting down speech. It can no longer be understood in its "everyday" or "ordinary" meaning of the simple transcription of spoken language. A distinction must now be made between the common, everyday, "narrow" and the radical, new, "enlarged" meaning of writing.

In its "narrow" meaning, as a simple notation technique, writing is derived from the speech it copies or records. Until now this "narrow" meaning obscured what Derrida proposes to name *arche-writing*, in reference to the "enlarged" meaning of writing. Derrida says that we continue to call arche-writing "writing,"

> only because it essentially communicates with the vulgar concept of writing. The latter could not have imposed itself historically except by the dissimulation of the arche-writing, by the desire for a speech displacing its other and its double and working to reduce its difference. If I persist in calling that difference writing, it is because, within the work of historical repression, writing was, by its situation, destined to signify the most formidable difference. It threatened the desire for living speech from the closest proximity, it *breached* living speech from within and from the very beginning.[16]

Arche-writing – the original trace, the deferment of presence and of living speech – is thus to be thought of as a "generalized"[17] writing that "covers the entire field of linguistic signs,"[18] in other words, the entire field of human activity. In fact, in so far as all cultures have the erasure or trace of presence as origin and any society "defers the proper" (including so-called societies "without writing"), grammatology must include the fields of anthropology, ethnology, and sociology.[19]

The point we must focus on here is the shift from

the narrow to the original meaning of writing. What authorizes this shift and how did it take place?

The shift is presented as a "modification." Derrida in fact speaks of a "modification of the concept of writing"[20] and later this "modification" is thought of as an "extension." But, as we have seen, it is in terms of its "enlarged" meaning that writing can be understood as "arche-writing." Derrida asks,

> Where does writing begin? When does writing begin? Where and when does the trace, writing in general, common root of speech and writing, *narrow itself* down into "writing" in the colloquial sense? Where and when does one pass from one writing to another, from writing in general to writing in the narrow sense, from the trace to the *graphie* and vice versa?[21]

The real challenge is to understand both the extent and the details of this "modification." Even if he never calls it such, it still appears that Derrida analyzes this modification as a *rewriting*. Caught in the hermeneutic circle engendered by the end of its metaphysical repression, writing would rewrite itself by enlarging its own meaning, as well as by bringing to light all the ramifications of its concept repressed by the logocentric tradition, and thereby claiming its own scope. In fact, reading *Of Grammatology*, it appears that there is no explanatory principle for the modification of writing to be found outside writing itself. This is confirmed at all three structural levels of the modification: the "automatic" enlargement of the meaning of writing born of the end of the metaphysical tradition; the way in which a schema impregnates an epoch (at a given moment writing is in the air, an urgent motif that demands priority in thought); the intervention of the philosopher who presents this hermeneutic as the work of writing.

(1) If arche-writing reveals what the logocentric repression hid, namely that writing refers not to a reproduction or imitation (of speech) but instead to a coincidence between the production and opening of difference, of all difference (hence the assimilation of arche-writing to difference),[22] then the meaning of writing would only enlarge itself in so far as it in fact rewrites itself, that is, in so far as it produces its own difference with itself.

Arche-writing reveals its trace as the narrowness of traditional writing appears. "Two writings" are not born in opposition as two constituted entities; rather the difference between two significations of writing engenders both. The enlarged meaning only has an "essence" in its difference from the narrow meaning. Hence the mode of meaning that derives its value from difference is precisely what Derrida names writing. Consequently, any modification (and not only of writing) produced by difference is a work of writing. The meaning of writing is thus enlarged by writing itself; it is released by deferring itself, by deconstructing itself, by ridding itself of the skin or corset of its traditional meaning. This, then, is eventually an automatic decompression writing.

(2) Moreover, this rewriting of writing, which makes freedom and the flipping of its concept possible, the shift from the everyday to the enlarged meaning, takes place in a historical context that Derrida says is marked by the pregnancy of the motif of writing in all fields of thought and practice. The transgression of logocentrism that is arche-writing cannot be thought without the here and now of a motif that imposes itself as the privileged instrument of interpretation of a culture at a particular moment in time.

Derrida explains the reason for this historic necessity very clearly. We are living, he explains in 1967, in the "epoch of writing" – which already implies the unavoidable change of meaning of this same term. This change is still only barely perceptible, but it is certain:

> By a slow movement whose necessity is hardly perceptible, everything that for at least some twenty centuries tended toward and finally succeeded in being gathered under the name of language is beginning to let itself be transferred to, or at least summarized under, the name writing. By a hardly perceptible necessity, it seems as though the concept

of writing – no longer indicating a particular, derivative, auxiliary form of language in general [. . .] is
beginning to go beyond the extension of language.[23]

We are beginning to "read otherwise," to "write
otherwise," and we speak of nothing but writing.
Writing is "in the air" or, as we say in French, writing
is "*l'air du temps*":

> Now we tend to say "writing" for all that and more:
> to designate not only the physical gestures of literal
> pictographic or ideographic inscription, but also the
> totality of what makes it possible; and also, beyond
> the signifying face, the signified face itself. And thus
> we say "writing" for all that gives rise to an inscrip-
> tion in general, whether it is literal or not and even
> if what it distributes in space is alien to the order of
> the voice: cinematography, choreography, of course,
> but also pictorial, musical, sculptural "writing." One
> might also speak of athletic writing and with even
> greater certainty of military or political writing in
> view of the techniques that govern those domains
> today. All this to describe not only the system of
> notation secondarily connected with these activities
> but the essence and the content of these activities
> themselves. It is also in this sense that the contempo-
> rary biologist speaks of writing and *pro-gram* in rela-
> tion to the most elementary processes of information
> within the living cell. And, finally, whether it has

essential limits or not, the entire field covered by the cybernetic *program* will be the field of writing.[24]

The semantic expansion of the concept of writing thus occurs in the real in a manner that is simultaneously diffuse and organized, beginning with the pregnant harboring of programming motifs (genetic and cybernetic), information and code. The real writes its own deconstruction. In other words, writing is *inscribed* in it, just as the genetic program is *inscribed* in cells. The impact of a book such as *The Logic of Life*,[25] by François Jacob, published in France just a few years after *Of Grammatology*, confirmed this emergence of writing in all fields of activity and thought, this grammatological structure of the being of an epoch. In the real of the 1960s, the "everyday" meaning was already "extending" itself. Jacob's book attests to the graphic power in the process of imposing itself, particularly in biology, through a privileged hermeneutical instrument, namely DNA, the genetic translation of an ontology of the graph that would now determine the understanding and study of life. The real writes itself.

(3) But the mere fact that writing is in the air is not enough to make it a grammatological epoch; it is still necessary to construct or elaborate grammatology itself, to construct or elaborate the meaning of writing as arche-writing. It is necessary to lend a hand to the automatic process, so to speak. This elaboration

---

of course requires the work and intervention of philosophers or, as Derrida would then say, "grammatologists." The task involves constituting writing as what I have called elsewhere a *motor scheme*, which corresponds, in another language, to the notion of "supplement."[26] Although writing is present everywhere, without this constitution it cannot designate a specific operation or structure, and hence it cannot be grasped by historical consciousness. In this way the illumination of arche-writing in Derrida is not only, as I have said, the result of an automatic freeing of the shackles of metaphysics, the somewhat natural end of a repression. It is also an invention born of a productive philosophical imagination. In the second part of *Of Grammatology*, Derrida demonstrates that the philosopher must be able to "open readings" of traditional texts; not content with commenting on them, by interpreting them the philosopher must "produce a signifying structure," one that the author did not necessarily perceive. In short, reading becomes a *rewriting* of texts.

The "modification" of writing can thus be understood as the synthesis of three movements, construed by Derrida as the operations of writing writ large: first, the automatic decompression of meaning that occurs with the closure of logocentrism (rewriting as the passage of writing in the narrow sense to arche-writing); second, the pregnancy of certain motifs in a context and a historical moment (the auto-inscription

---

of writing in *l'air du temps*); third, the invention and intervention of the philosopher who writes while reading. The modification is thus both the result of a non-mastery (automatism) and a mastery (scheme) of the structures of meaning, a combination made possible by the encounter of a certain state of these structures in the real (context).

Now you might ask whether these three axes in the modification of writing are really all of the order of writing. Do they not disarticulate at the very moment when we seek to bring them together, thus showing other principles of transformation?

By definition, what is in the air lasts only a moment in time. What would happen if writing (in both the narrow and enlarged senses) had come to the end of its time? And what would happen if the end of logocentrism was definitively over and had no more to release or free? Would that be the end of deconstruction? Or would we have to accept that *différance* continues, along with the modification of concepts, otherwise than as the work of writing or trace?

This point does not really seem to be examined in *Of Grammatology*. The assimilation of difference to writing, of alterity to writing, of modification to writing appears to be definitive. The tenacity of the trace also hides the historical variability of "supplementary" motifs.

And yet it is clear today that writing, as motor scheme, is no longer pregnant in the real. Writing is no longer the privileged hermeneutic stylus of the epoch. And as for the end of metaphysics or logocentrism, that's no longer current philosophy. What's left, then, of a supplement without its context, without its historical and ontological efficacy? What is a scheme without the concordance of the concept and the sensible? What does arche-writing become when writing no longer marks an epoch?

No supplement can claim to escape its own modification or substitution. Hasn't Derrida always recognized this, asserting as he did so clearly that a supplement only exists within a chain of substitutions – which implies that one day the supplement "writing" can and must give way to another? Despite everything – and this is the whole problem – according to Derrida this substitution structure can still be assimilated within the work of writing. The historical emergence of another supplementarity in no way invalidates the fact that, in principle, history, too, is writing:

> Historicity itself is tied to the possibility of writing; to the possibility of writing in general, beyond those particular forms of writing in the name of which we have long spoken of peoples without writing and without history. Before being the object of a history – of an historical science – writing opens the field of history – of historical becoming. [. . .] The history

of writing should turn back toward the origin of historicity.[27]

For Derrida, writing would thus also have the ability to include the potentially non-graphic nature of its becoming. And this is exactly what we must question today. Right from the start the impossibility of thinking the end of writing as privileged scheme or signifying structure threatens the grammatological project from within. This project can obviously neither produce nor understand the theory of its own replacement. And even if, through the impossible, grammatology could accord the change of supplement the status of a law, it would no longer be a grammatology, but rather a genetics of the formation of schema. Now, in as much as the emergence of a pregnant cultural motif, a scheme, or a supplement can only be grasped if the real offers it both echo and foundation, the theory of change of supplements can only deploy itself blow by blow and cannot actually constitute an autonomous epistemological field. *L'air du temps* can never be anticipated.

Here the question of *plasticity* unfurls. We no longer live in the epoch of writing. Each of the examples of the pregnancy of writing in the real presented in *Of Grammatology* and mentioned above could be discussed and deconstructed individually. In the field of genetics, for example, the motif of a code also experiences an "enlargement" of meaning.[28] In

---

cybernetics, "program" is no longer the key word. We are witnessing the decline of, or disinvestment in, the graph and graphics in general. Plastic images, presenting themselves as so many *figures* of self-organization, are tending to replace graphic images.

Neurobiology is no doubt the field in which the substitution of plasticity for writing is most evident. The models of *frayage* (facilitation), trace, and imprint are replacing models of form with neuronal configurations, network formations, and the emergence of assemblies. In this field it is striking to see how the concept of trace departs from a graphic understanding – as if traces no longer wrote. The example of the synaptic trace, that is, the result of recording experience at the level of neuronal connections, is most telling. Quantitative neuro-anatomic data now suggest that "neuronal assemblies," groups of cells that mutually engage and keep each other active, "code" experiences. Since Hebb's research we know that synapses are reinforced when the neurons they connect are frequently excited and mutually active. This "reinforcement" is materialized through a change in form. An accrued synaptic efficacy implies an increase in the size of neuronal networks, while a lesser efficacy (a "depression") leads to a reduction in the volume of networks. Such is the law of "synaptic plasticity."

In *Cortex: Statistics and Geometry of Neuronal Connectivity*, Valentino Braitenberg explains how the configurations formed by neuronal assemblies can be called "synaptic traces." He writes, "The basic tenet is that the "things" and "events" of our experience [. . .] do not correspond within the brain to individual neurons, but to groups of neurons called cell assemblies."[29] These groups may form in a single area of the brain, but they may also be formed through an overlap of different areas. The assemblies amount to "units of meaning as they appear as 'morphemes' in linguistics."[30] Neuronal assemblies would thus form a logic of signification, creating a "morphematic" distribution of the configurations at the root of our ideas.

Yet, despite everything, despite the borrowing of the linguistic and even grammatological model, the graphic trace does not coincide structurally with the synaptic trace. What Braitenberg and so many others since Hebb call a "trace" is a modification of form that corresponds to a plastic coding of experience, not to an imprint strictly speaking. Moving from the graphic to the plastic, the following are displaced: (1) the mode of deposit of the trace (what *leaving* a trace means); (2) the mode of distribution of meaning (do assemblies of neurons form a "text"?); (3) the mode of access to traces, in other words, interpretation (can neuronal plasticity really be "read" the way Freud said the unconscious could be read like a text?).

This passing reference to Freud is of course intentional. In "Freud and the Scene of Writing," Derrida shows that Freud confounds the mnesic trace with

59

the graphic trace. As a graphic trace, it has two main characteristics. First, the graphic trace is the result of a "*frayage*" or imprint: to leave a trace is to conquer the resistance of a material. Second, the graphic trace can become invisible, apparently disappear, giving the illusion of its erasure and thereby revealing the more ancient character of disappearance compared with disappeared presence.

Even if according to Derrida "psychic writing," as Freud construes it, is only a stage in the revelation of arche-writing, and even if Freud is faithful to a certain traditional determination of presence, the psychoanalytic concept of writing nonetheless contains the essential characterization of writing as "effraction," an inscription on a surface, a scratch or cut, a victory over the resistance of a material, the breaking open of a path – all of which are the definitions of writing to which Derrida remained true to the end:

> We ought thus to examine closely [. . .] all that Freud invites us to think concerning writing as "breaching" in the *psychical* repetition of this previously *neurological* notion: opening up of its own space, effraction, breaking of a path against resistances, rupture and irruption becoming a route *(rupta, via rupta)*, violent inscription of a form, tracing of a difference in a nature or a matter which are conceivable as such only in their *opposition* to writing. The route is opened in nature or matter, forest or wood

(*hylè*) and in it acquires a reversibility of time and space. We should have to study together, genetically and structurally, the history of the road and the history of writing.[31]

For Derrida one of the proofs that arche-writing remains essentially dependant on an understanding of the trace as a graphic inscription is the tenacity of the motif of *frayage*. Arche-writing must be understood (and can only be understood) in terms of *frayage*. As shown in the passage below, which includes no explicit reference to Freud and yet which is so close to the previous citation, "The Open Road" is the other title for *Of Grammatology*:

One should meditate upon all of the following together: writing as the possibility of the road and of difference, the history of writing and the history of the road, of the rupture, of the *via rupta*, of the path that is broken, beaten, *fracta*, of the space of reversibility and of repetition traced by the opening, the divergence from and the violent spacing, of nature, of the natural, savage, salvage forest. The *silva* is savage, the *via rupta* is written, discerned and inscribed violently as difference; as form imposed on the *hylè*, in the forest, in wood as matter; it is difficult to imagine that access to the possibility of a road-map is not at the same time access to writing.[32]

However, to return to the nature or structure of "neuronal morphemes," we must recognize that *frayage* is no longer a relevant category for thinking the synaptic "trace." Connections change form, but there is no route or breached material. Strictly speaking, nothing opens and the nervous influx does not carve out its wake. The synaptic trace does not proceed by cutting. The brain is not a wax tablet, nor is it a book.

The second characteristic of the graphic trace, in regard to its possible displacements or eclipses, is also troubled. The brain does not have the structure of a magic block. Neuronal networks do not form a palimpsest. Given the modifiable nature of synaptic efficacy, the coding of experience cannot be explained in terms of strata. The non-relevance of the *frayage* is accompanied by the non-relevance of the concept of stratification. Synaptic traces cannot be interpreted as rebuses, or as inscriptions in encoded language. The neurologist is not, or is no longer, an archeologist faced with a text that is not only half erased, but also written in several graphs, including the figurative, pictographic, ideographic, and linear, with all of these, as we have seen, spread out across several strata. The neurologist is not, or is no longer, a grammatologist.

Neuronal plasticity does not question the concept of trace – clearly there is a cerebral *différance* in the economy of situation, localization, structural relations, and the frequency of excitations – but it does challenge us to think a new, non-graphic meaning, as a result of *différance* itself.

The fact that plasticity is now in the air obviously has consequences for deconstruction, and this is the case as much in the progress of the movement of decompression of concepts as in the construction of supplementary schema by philosophers today. As we know, plasticity refers to a dual ability to receive form (clay is plastic) and give form (as in the plastic arts or plastic surgery). The deconstruction of concepts must therefore now be apprehended as a change of form, a metamorphosis. And all this also presupposes that the schema of writing gives way to a new schema in virtue of the very plasticity of its meaning, its modifiability, in a word, its aptitude for metamorphosis.

Because plasticity is now the privileged supplement/schema of our epoch, interrupting the tracing of the trace to replace it with the formation of form, it is clear that the expansion of the meaning of writing was already occurring in the non-written part of writing, in a transformation in which writing is but one instance. There is, in fact, a power to shape meaning that exceeds graphic displacement. The constitution of writing as a motor scheme is the result of a power of transformation of which grammatology is certainly but one instance. There is something other than writing in writing. And this "something other" is not speaking or presence. This non-graphic supplement that is plasticity does not introduce any logocentric remains, but rather marks dissidence from the grammatological instance in regard to itself while simultaneously identifying the dusk of its closure. Plasticity reveals an original modifiability of concepts in a supplementary manner without which the invention of arche-writing would not have been possible, but without which the invention of plasticity would not have been possible either. No paradigm of transformation has the value of a transcendental instance. By definition a supplement has no element, no origin, no essence, which is precisely why its destiny is that of constant change.

Another reason why a scientific grammatology never saw the light of day is that the operation of expanding concepts, including the concept of writing – whatever expansion this concept experiences – infinitely overflows the field of writing and cannot fix itself there. Just as the failure of general semiology can be explained by the impossibility of reducing linguistics to one of its areas, the failure of grammatology can be deduced from the royal share it grants writing. Grammatology cannot moderate the share of the graphic gesture, cannot limit its scope. In fact, in the science of writing it is impossible to produce the conditions of possibility of the plastic redevelopment of writing, in the same way that no "general plastology" could be integrated to the aging of plasticity. The plastic surgery of difference, deconstruction, and writing, which replaces rewriting, will likewise be only short-lived – a finite sublation.

But in retrospect this surgery reveals negatively a possibility that was abbreviated or even repressed by the graphic supplement and the assimilation without remains of difference, or of the *différance*, in regard to writing. This possibility is related to the transformation of form. It is true that the emergence of a supplement and its constitution as a motor scheme can obviously not occur except at the cost of repressing other "supplementary" possibilities. In the same way that the category of the "sign" in Saussure proceeds, as Derrida demonstrates, from a repression of writing, the notion of the graphic trace proceeds from a repression of form.

What does this mean? Do we seek to return to an evidence of form that would preside over the fate of the trace? Isn't plasticity always metaphysically delayed in relation to the play of writing or dissemination? If we claim that there is a non-graphic, that is, *plastic*, in the schematic construction of writing, isn't that to retain retrograde values, isn't that to make an attack on writing in the name of presence of the self to itself once again?

To this, I would first respond that a *non-metaphysical labor of form* is also experiencing its decompression or liberation today.[33] Second, plasticity is not, I repeat, an empty, transcendental instance. Plasticity is nothing outside its context and its supplementary status. The modifiability of concepts does not exist outside the specific historic modes of their modifications. The deformability or plasticity of a concept are no more ancient than the concept itself, they only reveal themselves in the act of a determined deformation. Just as the notion of the graphic trace is only a modality of the post-metaphysical future of philosophy – as was the linguistic sign reinterpreted by Saussure at another moment in time – plasticity will only last the time of its forms.

What then lies ahead, for philosophical creativity? The choice seems simple: either we recognize that deconstruction is dead and repeat that this is the case, or we accept the new change in modification, in other words, a change of difference. If the second option carries the day, then philosophical invention consists in refusing to repeat or pastiche a gesture that can no longer produce difference.

In *Margins of Philosophy*, Derrida writes, "I wish to underline that the efficacity of the thematic of *différance* may very well, indeed must, one day be superseded, lending itself if not to its own replacement, at least to enmeshing itself in a chain that in truth it never will have governed."[34]

We have come to the time for that replacement. Even if the chain of substitutes is not ready to cease, even if the plastic replacement will one day be sublated, our task now is to allow it to emerge. In other words, our task is to invent plasticity.

The phoenix, the spider, and the salamander[1]

To *recover*: this verb was at the heart of the questions Jacques Derrida asked me on December 15, 1994, the day of my doctoral defense, and that later appeared in his beautiful text "A Time for Farewells," published in French shortly after the thesis was published and accompanying the English translation.[2] Today I pay homage to his questions and to the dialogue we had that day. The discussion revolved around the meaning and scope of several of the gestures or movements contained in the verb "recover": to heal, to repair, to relocate a lost object or normal state, to reclaim, to recuperate.

My doctoral thesis focused on Hegel and the fundamental role of the concept of plasticity in Hegelian thought. The key question was whether, through the importance of this concept in dialectical temporality, plasticity could guarantee the existence of a true conception of the future in Hegel and, beyond that, a future for Hegelianism itself.

For Derrida, the first question was to describe a specific mode of philosophic invention. In this mode, invention does not lie in the creation of an entirely new concept or philosophical category, but rather in identifying a word or notion already present within a corpus, but to which no one has ever paid any attention. In this case, invention would consist not in forging a reading grid to be applied to the text, but rather in revealing the absolute singularity of a text starting with that which has been ignored within the text by readers and, to some extent, by author alike. Derrida referred to Deleuze's work on the notion of "expression" in Spinoza as a model for this approach, which consists in producing novelty by bringing back the ancient, revealing an unimagined force through the old text.

The concept of plasticity was long ignored by Hegel's critics and had never really been noticed by his commentators. Its sudden explosion after a long sleep therefore presents itself as a particular type of philosophical event situated between "recovery" or "rediscovery" and "discovery." In Derrida's words,

> To invent and most particularly understanding invention as an event, means here to rediscover what was there without being there, both in language and in philosophy; it is a question of finding, yes, but of finding for the first time what was always there and what had always been there, to find again, almost to re-find, something in its (contradictory) fusion and in its (atomic) fission where it had never before

been seen, to invent it almost, as one would invent a bomb, but to discover it also almost like the excessively obvious evidence of a purloined letter: never seen, never known, never waited on or for, never expected as such, while all the while only expecting it and not expecting anything else but it, the unexpected.[3]

Was it possible to invent Hegel by bringing him back? Was it possible to reinvent Hegel by healing him with a single word? One of the principal meanings of plasticity is the ability to recuperate . . . Was this kind of return, this plastic surgery, this "lifting," compatible with a new way of thinking?

More generally, does the intellectual decision to reawaken that which is already there lying dormant in language, lying hidden like a sleeping animal, does it really harbor genuine reserves for a future?

The letter will have been *there*, in other words, have been *truly* there in truth and if we reflect on this and read carefully what it means, it will have been there everywhere, everywhere where plasticity itself, everywhere where the lexicon and the concept of plasticity operates within the moments and the corpus of the history of philosophy, even before Aristotle and after Hegel, but especially in those towering figures, at the intersection of philosophy and science, of genetics and of politics, in

short, at the center of the *Encyclopedia*. To invent
and to formulate invention as an event, in this case,
is to find for the very first time and to show or
demonstrate what is there to be found within the
family, the genealogy, the resources of a lexicon and
by this gesture to institute, in a manner which shall
never again be effaceable, the modality in which
words become concepts and confirm thereby their
theoretical legitimacy. It is, in other words, formu-
lating the scene of an idiom as a philosophical *topos*
through which we will have to pass hereafter. Such
words which seemed lost, hidden away in language,
almost asleep in language, but asleep with one eye
open, here they appear leaping onto the center of
the stage, organizing and playing a lively and vigilant
role. These words are almost like animals.[4]

Do these returning words contain something that
Hegel still has to say to us and that has never yet been
spoken or heard?

The interesting point in this discussion is not,
or is not entirely, linked to the motifs of invention and recovery in general. It is also the question
of the determination of the two spaces assumed
by these operations: first, the space in which it is
brought back: "which is the scene of this good-bye
to which, without ever having said farewell, we are
now returning?";[5] second, the space arrived at after
such a leap. Clearly the conceptual animals Derrida

mentions do not come from just any forest, nor are they ready to leap into just any scene. They claim to breach two limits and this is the claim Derrida examines.

In order for any philosophical invention worthy of its name to arise, concepts must first cross the limit of traditional metaphysics. They must reach the space beyond-enclosure of tradition. To invent is to cross this first limit, the limit Heidegger compares, in the *Principle of Reason*, to the ring of fire tigers leap through.[6] If a concept or philosophical thought are able to return, to recover their vitality, that is, their future, then they must do it *from* the end of metaphysics, they must be able to leap through this ring. It is therefore important to ask whether plasticity and, beyond it, Hegel's philosophy itself, can cross this line.

The second frontier is deconstruction. Even if Hegel is able to return, in the name of or in virtue of his plasticity, he must also be able to cross the ring of fire of his own deconstruction. After all, you can hardly write a thesis on the recuperative abilities (plasticity) of Hegel under the direction of the author of *Glas* without risking the hypothesis of such supersession. Hegel must be able to get back up (*relever*) from the deconstruction of sublation (*relève*).

Invention as rediscovery consists therefore not only in awakening authors and philosophical categories that were thought complete, over, worn out by tradition, but also in re-launching them beyond their deconstruction. The question Derrida asks is what chance does a philosopher like Hegel, or a word like plasticity, have of returning from both metaphysics *and* the deconstruction of metaphysics? Coming from this scene, can plasticity enable philosophy to heal from both metaphysics and the sound of its tolling bell? To bring back is not to repeat, is not to mime, is not to reproduce. By bringing back Hegel and the concept of plasticity, clearly it is not a question of following the fantasy of rediscovering them intact, untouched by deconstruction; on the contrary, it is about imagining the way in which they can rebound from their dual situation in tradition and in deconstruction.

As Derrida understood perfectly well, this is also to say that alongside the future of Hegel, the plastic way of philosophizing puts at stake the future of deconstruction. Again, and in the same way, when it is a question today of measuring the legacy of Derrida, of recovering what he left to share with the future, it is not about repeating him, miming him, or reproducing him. It is a question of inventing deconstruction from the place of an internal dissidence, the secret and sometimes unthought announcement of a separation of *différance* with itself, which alone can engage it with its posterity.

To recover: how does this movement inscribe itself in the mobility of deconstruction if it claims to exceed it? To bring it back and to differ: do these two metabolic operations follow an identical wake or do they separate exactly at the point of this question, namely the trace?

To bind together all these questions, I chose to interpret the famous statement in *Phenomenology of Spirit*: "The wounds of the Spirit heal and leave no scars behind."[7]

In this passage Hegel is talking about the beautiful soul which, always ready to forgive, to forget faults, perpetually returns to itself, rediscovers itself, reconstitutes itself, recuperates. It is possible to see in this phrase the very definition of the work of the spirit. It expresses precisely this process of recovery, healing, return, the re-knitting of the skin after the wound, in other words, the plasticity that appears as the very movement of the absolute.

There are three possible interpretations of this phrase. A dialectical-metaphysical interpretation, a deconstructive interpretation, and a third that I'll provisionally call post-deconstructive. The first ring of fire (metaphysics/deconstruction) lies between the first and second interpretation, while the second ring of fire (deconstruction/post-deconstruction) lies between the second and third. Each of these three readings is based on a specific understanding of healing, reconstitution, return, and regeneration. These readings mobilize three paradigms of recovery:

the paradigm of the *phoenix*, the paradigm of the *spider*, and the paradigm of the *salamander*.

Tracking these animals, the confrontation of the three structures of the wound, the inscription, and healing, would allow us to re-launch the question of "bringing back" and recovery, starting with a specific understanding of the erasure of the trace or the scar.

The paradigm of the phoenix, the legendary bird that Hegel compared to the spirit, illustrates or incarnates the movement of absolute presence constantly reconstituting itself from its wounds. Here regeneration and recovery are confounded with the process of dialectical sublation (*Aufhebung, la relève*). Rent in two, the spirit constantly returns to itself and leaves no trace of the tear. Like the phoenix, the spiritual, Hegel says "eternally preparing for itself its funeral pyre, and consuming itself upon it; but so that from its ashes is produced the new, renovated, fresh life."[8] Citing Hegel's article on *Natural Law*, Derrida declares that "in this text, the name of what takes wing again [*reprendre son vol*] is neither the owl nor the eagle, but the phoenix: starting with its consuming destruction, life "as its own seed-corn (*als sein eigenes Samenkorn*)" "rise[s] (*emporhebe*) eternally . . . from its ashes to new youth."[9] In the paradigm of the phoenix, true regeneration is resurrection. The fabled phoenix, endowed with the power to be reborn from its ashes and thus with immortality, symbolizes the labor of the spirit that returns to itself from extreme rending. In this

74

first paradigm "to recover" means "to be present once again," to return to the scene. Healing implies a reconstitution of wounded presence, an annulment of the defect, the mark, the lesion. To describe this type of recovery Hegel thus refers to the metaphor of the skin that regenerates without leaving a scar. The image of this return to and on the self also appears at the end of the *Phenomenology of Spirit*, in the metaphor of the liquid which, pouring on the ground as it overflows from the chalice, splashes back up and refills it anew.[10]

In Hegel the trace, the wound, and its healing are submitted to the authority of the "value of presence."[11] The disappearance or erasure of the scar coincides with the appearance of the spirit. Healing is a disappearance that presents itself, a *phenomenology*.

For Hegel wounds are but preliminaries in a reconstitution of the identical in the organ that is damaged or destroyed. Separation, suffering, rending mark only ephemeral periods of gaping. The negative constantly prepares its own regeneration. Negativity is the act of "its own restless process of sublating itself."[12] Dialectical plasticity is the constant reconstitution of presence that finds the resources of its youth or health each time in a higher form of life.

In some ways the paradigm of the spider, which corresponds to the weaving of the web or the text and symbolizes deconstruction here, is also a structure of erasure of the trace. But far from permitting the

75

return of an intact, undamaged presence, this type of erasure marks precisely the originary impossibility of presence to be anything other than a trace. In "Différance," Derrida writes:

> Since the trace is not a presence but the simulacrum of a presence that dislocates itself, displaces itself, refers itself, it properly has no site. Erasure belongs to its structure. And not only the erasure which must always be able to overtake it (without which it would not be a trace but an indestructible and monumental substance), but also the erasure which constitutes it from the outset as a trace, which situates it as the change of site and makes it disappear in its appearance, makes it emerge from itself in its production.[13]

We must therefore distinguish two conceptions of erasure. If the scar is construed as that which bears witness to the presence of the wound, the presence of the past, then it seems that *différance* also leaves no scar, in that it is neither past nor present. In fact, again, as Derrida writes, "The concept of trace is incompatible with the concept of retention, of the becoming-past of what have been present. One cannot think the trace – and therefore *différance* – on the basis of the present."[14]

And yet the tissue, the web of the text are covered with marks, nicks, scratches that are so many scars of the impossibility of reconstituting the origin or taking on a new skin. These marks, however, do not show themselves and do not promise any vestige.

Thus the infamous "spelling mistake" that led to writing "*différance*" with an *a* is really a wounding of language, which retains the scar of this "infraction." However, this legible, but inaudible error, "remains silent, secret, and discreet as a tomb."[15] The scar of removing the "e" disappears as soon as the word is pronounced *différance*. But at the same time, this *a* hides nothing and promises no revelation nor any truth:

> Reserving itself, not exposing itself, in regular fashion [*la différance*] exceeds the order of truth at a certain and precise point, but without dissimulating itself as something, as a mysterious being, in the occult of a nonknowledge or in a hole with indeterminable borders (for example in a topology of castration). In every exposition it would be exposed to disappearing as disappearance. It would risk appearing: disappearing.[16]

As we know, *différance* has no essence and "is" not. This is why its paradigm is the text, the multiple links of the network or tissue of letters that cannot be left to reach a non-textual presence. If the text is cut, the section creates still more text. The tissue reweaves itself from its torn pieces, creating an entanglement of veils. But in this constant regeneration, it is not the skin that grows back identical; no growth of presence closes the wound or corrects the faults. It is the tissue of the text that expands, becomes more complex and ramifies without ever achieving the proof of a definitive form.

To say therefore that a trace only manages to erase itself is to say that this erasure must also be a mark. A trace can only ever erase itself, but in turn erasure can only ever leave a trace. For Derrida, all the meanings of the verb "recover" are understood in terms of the tissue-text. The tissue is both web and living tissue. Reading, understanding, interpreting are decisive acts of cutting that provoke wounds in the tissue and the flesh everywhere, slashing and gashing. The text always reconstitutes itself, retaining the prints and traces of all the readings and acts of the spirit. In *Dissemination*, Derrida describes the text as "reconstituting it too as an organism, infinitely regenerating its own tissue behind the cutting trace, the decision of each reading."[17] Here the regeneration of the living tissue coincides with the process of scarring and the inscription of the memory of the wound. In fact, Derrida wrote *Glas* in the name of this sort of arrangement of multiple inscriptions, both uneffaceable and erased. Writing versus resurrection.

As we see, regeneration does not correspond at all here to the return of eternal youth of the phoenix. Rather, it refers to the constant return of the web, the repair, the lucky chance. Healing is therefore uncertain, the remedy may create another lesion, the sewing of the text can fray, opening other craters, other holes.

To return to our invention, it is a matter of knowing whether plasticity, to which Hegel was the first philosopher to accord the value of a concept, can have any meaning outside the "value of presence." Can plasticity also describe the graft, the mending of the tissue or the text? Apparently not. In "A Time for Farewells . . ." Derrida shows that the reconstitution of tissue or web resists plastic regeneration, which he claims is always attached to salvation or to redemption. He says that *différance* is a "'salutation' that must begin by refusing all the assurances of salvation," that it "renounces the possibility of 'seeing again,' which unequivocally relinquishes or abandons the assurance of repetition or of redemption [. . .]."[18]

Derrida himself never stops rediscovering, recovering, bringing back concepts lost in language. He also revives the singularity of texts from their silence or inertia due to the passing of time. But the mode of return that he instigates is not true plasticity. According to him, plasticity always follows an "interiorizing, incorporating, *sublating*, idealizing, spiritualizing"[19] movement. In short, for Derrida plasticity is always dialectical. How could Hegel surmount such an observation? Derrida adds: the more the salutation is "assured or given [. . .], the more the promise becomes a calculation, that is, the more it is lost – as future."[20]

"The wounds of the Spirit heal and leave no scars behind": between the two possible interpretations of this phrase, between presence and tissue, it would now no longer be possible to pass through the ring of fire. How could we bring Hegel, or plasticity, back, other than as ghosts?

Unless there is a third way. Beyond the dialectical and "differential" or textual meaning of healing, the third reading of the phrase in *Phenomenology of Spirit*, would follow this other way. The way of the salamander . . .

My research on plasticity led me to an interest in "regenerative" medicine, which develops a set of auto-repairing or self-regenerating techniques for organs and tissues.

This type of medicine takes advantage of the astounding possibilities of stem cells. Scientists are working on totipotent embryonic stem cells which differentiate themselves to give birth to all of the types of cells in an organism, as well as on adult stem cells, non-specialized cells found in specialized tissues (the brain, bone marrow, blood, blood vessels, the retina, liver . . .). During renewal most of these cells generate cells that are similar to the cells of the tissue from which they come. But scientists have discovered that some of them (notably skin stem cells) can transform into other types of cells (nerve or muscle cells, for instance). This process is called "trans-differentiation." Starting with these cells it is therefore possible to manufacture skin, muscle, neurons, to regenerate the sick organ without the aid of outside intervention. This type of medicine is called regenerative medicine because of the ability of certain animals to re-engender one or several damaged or amputated body parts. The salamander is the most well-known and spectacular example, for it can regenerate members (limb, tail) and portions of organs, such as the eye or the heart. Through the use of stem cells, regenerative medicine today tends to rediscover this self-repairing faculty inscribed in the memory of species. It is increasingly common to use regeneration in the treatment of coronary thrombosis, burns, or Parkinson's disease . . .

These new therapeutic possibilities – which only emerged in the late 1990s – invite philosophical reflection in many ways. In particular they lead us to understand Hegel's phrase in a new light. When a salamander or lizard's tail grows back we do indeed have an instance of healing without a scar. The member reconstitutes itself without the amputation leaving any trace. Yet it seems to me that this phenomenon of recovery is not readable in terms of the dialectic reinterpreted through the *différance* or the logic of the text. It is not about a sublation or about a sewing back. This regeneration is neither a resurrection nor a graft; it is without a *pharmakon* and without an intruder.

What comes, or comes back, after the dialectic and after the text, proceeding from a very ancient memory, one still more ancient than that of metaphysics, the memory of the living? What does this archaic plasticity that invents itself by returning teach us?

Cell biology proves the possibility of a dissociation between regeneration and immortality. When the hydra is cut in two, it proves to be capable of regenerating an entire animal starting with each of the two divided parts. If some worms are chopped up, each bit engenders a new organism that is identical to the original. Regeneration is in fact cloning. At the edge of its reproductive processes the animal is liable to find in itself the possibility of repair through replication.

I repeat: in all the instances cited above, the wounds leave no scars. When a lizard's tail grows back, it leaves no trace of the amputation at all. But this phenomenon does not correspond to dialectical sublation as defined earlier. The organ reconstitutes itself without scars, but this healing does not raise life to a form of completion. The organ that grows back is indeed different from the one it replaces – in size, weight, form. The regenerated limb of the salamander is often smaller than the first. This difference is neither a form of higher life nor a monstrous gap. It is a *finite* reconstitution, a resurrection without miracle or parousia. There is no scar, but there is difference.

This, then, is what separates the salamander from the phoenix. The phoenix is reborn from its ashes while remaining eternally identical to itself. The salamander is mortal and reconstitutes itself in an incompressible difference with itself. The limb that grows back never looks the same as the one that was lost, although it is perfectly identical structurally. Regeneration is therefore not a reconstitution of presence, but rather a regeneration of difference. Here "to recover" implies a finite survival, a momentary resource. The regrowth does not annul finitude; rather it is one of its expressions.[21] In this sense, regeneration is certainly in the order of what Derrida called a supplement, a stranger to the value of presence, to "self-interrelating with its own difference."[22]

The problem is that this supplement exceeds or displaces the logic of *différance* while also troubling the second interpretation of our initial phrase, the one that mobilizes the paradigm of the web.

Let us continue the biological investigation. With humans, as with all mammals, regeneration is practically extinct. Only a few rare instances of the regenerative capacities of the salamander or the hydra persist: the epidermis and blood vessels tend to reconstitute themselves only when they are damaged; in some instances the liver can self-regenerate; the last phalanx can grow back on children and adolescents. But these possibilities are extremely limited and appear to be the vestiges of an immemorial past.

Why did regeneration die out? This is an interesting point: it seems that in the course of evolution scarring replaced regeneration. In higher-order animals, it is less advantageous to leave a wound open for a long period than for it to scar over. Apparently evolution pushed aside regeneration among superior animals because it takes longer than scarring and represents a less advantageous and less costly factor of adaptation. Scarring is thus a mode of healing that came late in the history of species.

Clearly the scar is a physical obstacle to regeneration, since it forms a crust or fibrous shell that prevents the reconstitution of the member or damaged organ.

What happens if the limb of a salamander is cut off? The epidermic cells migrate rapidly to the surface of the stump and cover it over entirely with a sort of envelope. When the amputated surface is totally re-covered a second phase, known as "de-differentiation," begins. Under this envelope, the stem cells that had differentiated themselves into nervous, muscular, or vascular cells lose their specialization. They dedifferentiate themselves and form a type of bud, the regenerative blastema, from which, through a process of trans-differentiation, they regenerate the entire amputated structure. No scar is formed. The wound heals and leaves no scar behind. Among mammals, on the other hand, this blastema does not form; in its place appears the scar.

Today regenerative medicine is based essentially

on the possibility of reactivating these lost functions, which implies inhibiting the scarring process. This inhibition or erasure is possible in two ways: through the activation of the dedifferentiation and trans-differentiation of stem cells (therapeutic cloning) and through the neutralization of scarring genes (a function of gene therapy).

Biologists are therefore working today to redis-cover the trace of the same process of erasure of the trace or the scar. With the instigation of the paradigm of the salamander by contemporary biology, we face a dual process of disappearance of the trace. First, the disappearance linked to natural regeneration: the limb or tissue reconstitutes itself, there is no scar, the mark of the wound is erased. Second, the disappearance of the scarring process itself, a disappearance provoked by medical technique. It is a matter of erasing the mark that obliterates a very ancient process of erasing the mark.

Once again, natural and artificial or technical regeneration do not introduce the "value of pres-ence." One might say that stem cells are "present" in the organism in the same way a potential that may always be activated is present, in the same way the slumbering animals mentioned at the beginning of this text lie ever ready to leap. But just like these animals, they can also surprise us by leaping up and through the ring of fire, transgressing the limit. Stem cells are only present in the form of explosive reserves of presence, which can completely disrupt teleology. Ready at any moment to change difference, they lie in the organism as a possible resource, at the threshold of their future roles.

The paradigm of the salamander is not only irreducible to the structure of sublation or dialectical resurrection, it is also irreducible to the paradigm of tissue. The salamander does not allow itself to be entirely caught up in the folds of the text. It heals by erasing writing.

The salamander reminds us, in fact, that regeneration is a de-programming, an "un-writing" if you will. Stem cells can *change difference*, change inscription. Regenerative medicine proves the outdated nature of a belief that was held until very recently, namely, the irreversibility of cellular differentiation and genetic programming. Today biologists use the concept of *plasticity* to refer to the ability of cells to modify their program, to change their text.

The therapeutic and ontological work of plasticity thus upsets both the dialectical work of self-repair of the absolute as well as the motifs of writing and textuality in general. Here, repair does not derive from the same or from the entirely other. Due to this complexity, it does not only appear as the supplement of the supplement, as a simple replacement of writing. It no longer belongs to the era of metaphysics, it also announces a change of regime of the supplement itself.

Unlike the regeneration of the spirit in Hegel and unlike the displacement of the letter in Derrida, plasticity takes sublation and regenerates it as supplementarity. I call plasticity *the resistance of différance to its graphic reduction*. Or, if you will, that which, in *différance*, is not present but which does not write itself either. Something that is not present, that is not absent, that is not written.

In some ways Derrida himself gradually abandoned, or at least transformed, the imperative to deconstruct presence. In his books, readings of the traditional major philosophers became more infrequent and rare. The opposition between the phoenix and the spider's web becomes less insistent. In time the key question metamorphoses and regenerates itself. As proof, I'll mention the emergence of the problem of the "undeconstructible," that Derrida outlined in his late work under the names of "justice" or "democracy."[23] If there are un-deconstructible cases then that means that they can come back, that in a certain sense they cross the two rings of fires that are the history of metaphysics and the era of deconstruction. The un-deconstructible is not of the order of presence, but it is just as much a form of resistance to the text. Derrida therefore had to admit that there was a form of substance that, without being a parousia, can no longer be confused with the incessant mobility of graphic difference. It appears, however, that for lack of time he did not sufficiently examine the ontological consistency of the un-deconstructible. Would he have been willing to see in it the secret of the salamander?

To my mind, this is the essential question Derrida bequeaths us. But who's to say that Hegel did not ask it? Philosophical texts are returning today as we have never before seen them, reconstituting themselves from their deconstruction. They bear no scar, yet they are no longer the same, but nor are they other. Neither the same nor unrecognizable, they are clones of themselves that open up new resources to thought. After all, isn't cloning one of the possible meanings of absolute knowledge?

"The wounds of the spirit heal and leave no scars behind": what is the real meaning of "recovery" in this phrase? Presence? Writing? Regeneration? In "A Time for Farewells . . .," Derrida makes a beautiful admission: "It is as though, in history, in my history, a strange accident happened to the word accident (and hence to the word essence), an accident of which I am no longer sure, of which no one can be sure of being able to *sublate*."[24]

This admission supports the dialectical meaning of plasticity. But who is to say that regenerative plasticity does not eventually speak to us today of the accidents without essence that repair themselves without salvation, regeneration without sublation? And who says that Hegel could not see them coming?

The phoenix, the spider, and the salamander

What does the departed leave in me? A presence, a trace or a difference without a scar? It is for me to decide between these three the meaning, between essence and accident, of "the time for farewells."

Woman's possibility, philosophy's impossibility

This may be the most abominable affair in criminal history of all times: at Ciudad Juárez, a border town in the North of Mexico, the twin city of El Paso (Texas), more than 300 women have been murdered, all following the same ritual of kidnap, torture, sexual services, mutilations, strangulation. For ten years on average two bodies have been found every month in the surroundings of the accursed city – the naked, bruised, disfigured bodies of women, adolescents and young girls. Top-level investigators believe it is the work of two psychopathic "serial killers," but no one can find them . . .

Sergio González Rodríguez,
Le Monde Diplomatique, August 2003.

There has been a lot of talk about Mr. Zapatero's promise to withdraw Spanish troops from Iraq, but in Spain thousands of women are waiting for him to hold firm on another promise: to implement a law against "domestic violence." Every day in Spain we read about cases of murder or violence

90

against women in the newspaper, but these stories
do not figure among the minor news items hidden
inside the paper, they're on the front page and
in the headlines of television news reports. With
more than seventy women murdered by their hus-
bands or ex-husbands last year, this is definitely an
urgent issue for the Spanish. Last year fifty thousand
women reported an attack to the law and in each
of these instances the aggressor was a spouse or
ex-spouse.

Les femmes en Espagne, France 5
television channel, February 2009.

According to figures published in 2006 by the
French Ministry of Labor, women's wages are on
average 73 percent of those of men right across different work schedules (*Les écarts de salaire entre les
hommes et les femmes en 2006: des disparités persistantes*
[Salary gaps between men and women in 2006:
persistent disparities]). (1) The total gap: women
received 27 percent less. [. . .] (2) The gap for full-
time work: women receive 19 percent less. The first
explanation for these wage inequalities is different
work structures. Women are five times more likely
to work part-time than men; consequently, their
income for all work schedules is less than the income
received by men. Furthermore, men's work time is
increased through the overtime they receive more
frequently than women. (3) The gap for equivalent

91

positions and experience: women receive 10 percent
less. If differences in position (manager, employee,
worker), experience, qualification (degree level) and
activity sector (education or finance) are taken into
account, some 10 percent of the gap remains inex-
plicable. This difference in treatment amounts to
a degree of *pure* employer discrimination against
women. However, other factors that are not meas-
ured can be at work here and may partially explain
the phenomenon, starting with family situation,
degree subject and career breaks. Pure discrimination
probably amounts to 6 or 7 percent. But discrimination also shows in other areas, in part-time work and
getting stuck in low-level or low-paid jobs.

Observatoire des inégalités, January 6, 2009.

Still today the professional or personal achievements
of a woman cannot be seen as anything other than
an act of emancipation. Whether or not this achieve-
ment is accompanied by activist demands, it is always
political. Clearly, to be a woman still means to belong
to a category that is dominated sexually, symbolically,
socially, economically, and culturally. Consequently,
whenever a woman succeeds in establishing her crea-
tions in any field, she is contributing to improving the
lot and future of all women. Although a new radical-
ism has made it necessary to question the ontological,
political, and biological meanings of "woman," the
word is still attached – perhaps now more than ever

– to the historical schema of the march towards liberation, towards a specific liberation that cannot be confounded with other liberations. Even as we question the identity "woman," it is inconceivable that the tenacity of "feminist" demands be forgotten for a moment. The deconstruction of sexual identities does not imply letting go of the fight for women's liberation.

I am not being naïve in introducing my topic like this. I speak fully aware of what remains of the feminine after its deconstruction. The word "remains," echoing the famous "what remains of absolute knowledge?" in *Glas*, does not refer to any sort of debris, be it bones or ashes. It refers not to a residue but to a kernel of resistance, a kernel with the strength of a new beginning, a live instance that still burns – quite the opposite of a broken limb or cadaver. The beginning of a new fire; the prelude to new forms. Although I have questioned the coincidence of woman and the feminine, notably in "The Meaning of the 'Feminine'," I did so knowing that there is a secret plasticity in both woman and the feminine as they come into a new era today, an era that opens up to them as a direct result of their post-deconstructive meaning.

I propose a minimal concept for woman, an ineffaceable "remains" in which "woman" refers to a subject overexposed to a specific type of violence. This violence can be defined fundamentally as a dual constraint or schizoid pressure: the pressure of work in society and at home. This minimal concept – woman's overexposure to dual exploitation – is the remainder, burning and plastic, with which we must work.

While we know that the constitution of any gender identity involves power play, that it always imposes itself within opposing strengths, we must also acknowledge the specificity of violence to women. Although this violence shares features with other types of oppression, it is nonetheless irreducible. The dual constraint of work inside and outside the home, with all of the inequality, humiliation, conjugal mistreatment, sexual abuse, beating, murder, and its ideological status as a shameful problem, threatens women in a specific way.

Even when a theorist such as Beatriz Preciado asserts the existence of a dissemination of sexual difference, reflecting the emergence of unexpected identities, of "queer multitudes," and claims that "if the queer multitudes are post-feminist, it is in so far as they are the result of a reflexive confrontation of feminism and the differences it erased to the advantage of a hegemonic, heterocentric political subject 'woman'," she recognizes that domestic violence most often affects women or "feminized bodies."[1]

And here comes the immediate objection: isn't defending the specificity of this violence simply a fall-back to a form of essentialism that confers a determinate identity on "woman"? To this I respond that what I mean by "woman" is not the subject of traditional feminism at war with "male domination." Yes, it is necessary to break with "all essentialist feminism,"[2] but at the same time let's admit that the fierce battle waged within various feminist movements between "essentialism" and "anti-essentialism" – the label "essentialist" is attached to any discourse that tries to identify anything like a specificity of the feminine – loses its meaning and ultimately turns against feminist efforts. While we must avoid all essentializing of the feminine, we must also critique, with equal vehemence, as Naomi Schor commented in the early 1990s, the "excesses perpetrated in the name of anti-essentialism," when she stated loud and clear "the urgency of rethinking the very terms of a conflict which all parties would agree has ceased to be productive."[3]

This is why the notion of "essence" must be reexamined, and that is exactly what I intend to do here, not through a process of heavy ontological enquiry, but by asking whether this term is correctly understood by those who malign it. I want to keep hold of the thought of the specificity of the violence to women, even at the risk of taking on a form of acceptance of essence that has nothing to do with what feminist theorists usually understand by this term.

To meet these goals, I must start by identifying the intersection between two explicit gestures to de-essentialize "woman": the first is philosophical, undertaken by deconstruction, while the second, which is critical and pragmatic, is undertaken by gender studies and queer theory. These two approaches are far from identical, which is why their meeting point is not always clearly perceived or understood. Consideration of this encounter reveals that a kind of anti-essentialist violence can play into the hands of ordinary violence against women in both the domestic and social realm. As if deconstruction and gender theory on the one hand and the murderous impulse and material violence on the other ultimately share a little something in regard to "woman," a little of her flesh or lips. As if they both, as it were, take their payment in kind and share the spoils.

It is certainly right to state firmly that the de-ontologizing operation at work in theory and philosophy is irreducible to any kind of terrorism. But even if it is only to reject it, we cannot avoid questioning the complicity between a domestic and social violence that refuses to give women a place and a theoretical violence that refuses to give women an essence.

In gender studies "essence" often refers to a combination of natural, biological, or anatomical determinants (all three are treated as synonymous) – the woman's "sex," her "body" – and a given social construction, feminine identity as it appears as a product of the heterosexual ideological matrix. Both natural determination and social construction refer to a supposedly stable and unchanging essence. To speak of the "specificity" of the feminine would be essentialist, since this discourse could only be a reclaiming of the "proper," a preordained anatomical and cultural reality. Few feminist theorists seem to question the crude amalgam that such an understanding of essence conveys, one that reduces biology to nothing more than the science of constituted identities and culture to a movement to re-appropriate these identities for normalizing ends.

The anti-essentialism of "queer multitudes" emphasizes the infinite, unlimited, horizontal mutability and transformability of bodies, behavior, and gender, as if this constant displacement were able to eradicate the supposed stability of essence by itself. As I demonstrated in "The Meaning of the 'Feminine'," anti-essentialism never exactly questions the proximity of the two concepts of "gender," the first of which refers to essence in the philosophical sense (*genre*) and the second of which refers to sexual identity (*gender*). As if, between genre and gender, the identity of the word and its root were no more than a coincidence.

In deconstruction the concept of essence relates, first, in a far more rigorous manner, to its ontological meaning as the "form" or "idea" of a thing. But essence never transgresses these metaphysical boundaries. For Derrida, form or essence refer to presence, the evident, *parousia*, and signify only within the metaphysical tradition, that is, ontology. Form and essence have no post–deconstruction future.

If, as I have just explained, we must clarify the intersection of gender theory and deconstruction, it is in so far as whatever the difference of their approaches, there nonetheless appears to be a consensus regarding a definition of essence as stability, self-presence, and nature, in both the ontological and biological meaning of the term.

How can we elude this kind of alliance? How can we defend the specificity, however unstable, however relative, of a violence done to women if the very notion of "specificity" is subject to the counter-violence of a constant de-appropriation?

That "woman" is now emptied of her essence only serves to emphasize the fact that she does not define herself and cannot define herself except through the violence done to her. Violence alone confers her being. The violence of the deconstruction of this being, on the one hand, and, on the other, the domestic and social violence constantly exerted on this very absence of being. Woman is nothing any more, except this violence through which her "being nothing" continues to exist. She's nothing but an ontological amputation, formed by that which negates her.

This assimilation of "woman" to "being nothing" perhaps opens a new path that goes beyond both essentialism and anti-essentialism. Let us envisage the possibility that, in the name woman, there is an empty but resistant essence, an essence that is resistant precisely because it is emptied, a *stamp of impossibility*. This could augur a new era in the "feminist" fight, a new stage in the battle against the violence that claims woman is impossible because of her lack of essence.

To answer these questions, I'll start by analyzing my own situation, which has the advantage of being positioned exactly at the articulation of the registers at stake here. Indeed, since I am a philosopher, my work, in the economic and social meaning of the term, and my material position in the community coincide with my intellectual engagements and, in particular, with my interest in gender theory and deconstruction. I confront domestic/social violence as an individual and as a working woman, while I also confront the theoretical violence of the de-ontologizing of woman. Setting aside women and violence in general, I'll start with the individual situation of a "female professional philosopher," who, aside from institutional bullying of all kinds, has had to face in the past and sometimes still faces, the pressures of daily life, the threats of symbolic punishment, the refusal of *jouissance* or freedom, inequality or insidious forms of injustice.

What is the life of a woman philosopher? In line with the project of resistance announced earlier, I'll try to show first what woman – or what's left of her

– renders definitively impossible in the philosophical sphere that has always excluded her violently. Then, in conjunction with this, I'll try to imagine what woman – or what's left of her – renders definitively impossible in gender and queer theory. As a fugitive of lightness (emptied of essence), "woman" transforms her nothing of essence into a final vanishing point outside an overly narrow and excessively violent, philosophical, and critical determination of essence. As a fugitive of lightness (emptied of essence), for a long time now "woman" has brought her body with her, leaving anti-essentialists to their (real) phantasy of a determined biological and anatomical body, a body beaten again and again.

I'll start by pointing out the inanity of the concept "woman philosopher." Since the identity this phrase suggests does not exist. This statement can be understood in two contradictory ways. First, the inexistence of the woman philosopher is a consequence of the philosophical violence exerted on women who are not considered subjects. Second, in counterpoint to the first definition, the inexistence of the woman philosopher is the result of a battle and a decision by women themselves. In what follows, I'll explain how these two meanings are interwoven.

Philosophy is woman's tomb. It grants her no place, no space whatsoever, and gives her nothing to conquer. As we know, the European philosophical tradition is a tradition based on the exclusion of woman; it belittles her and is thereby complicit in the worst macho violence. Women philosophers are not convincing and continue to be exploited as non-subjects, at least symbolically. Nothing in the metaphysical genealogy is open to them on their terms. The possibility of philosophy is thus largely premised on the impossibility of woman.

The violence women suffer in this field is not just physical. Nevertheless, the scorn, the inequity in symbolic status, the lack of recognition that women experience within the institution, as well as sometimes at home with their partners and families, make this violence a pressure that it would be difficult not to consider as "physical." It's a painful burden, in that it cannot be relieved using the same weapons from which it is made, namely philosophy. In France, despite their financial autonomy, level of education, skills, and the apparent ease of their work in and outside the home, women philosophers who are researchers, academics, high school teachers, or independent scholars, either outside the institution or on its margins, have never been able to bring into being what might properly be called a "feminine philosophy."

I am speaking here about France in particular because the situation and institutional definition of philosophy is different here from that of other countries. Yet even in the Anglo-American tradition, in so-called "analytic" philosophy, there is virtually no "specifically" feminine philosophical tradition. Women do not do "women's" philosophical work.

I hear the questions already: what do you mean by "women's philosophy"? Isn't the "proper" the first value to deconstruct? Isn't the difficulty you emphasize also inherent in fields other than philosophy? No doubt it is. And it's true that I would have some difficulty in giving a clear definition of this "authenticity or property." Yet it is absolutely clear to me that in the whole field of philosophy, there is still no equivalent to a Marguerite Duras in literature, a Pina Bausch in dance, or a Georgia O'Keeffe in painting. No doubt it would be difficult to say in these instances, too, how exactly these women do *authentically* "feminine" work. Yet it seems indisputable that they do change the given rules of their art, they transform the stakes and engender a tradition, and that, for the time being, this has never yet happened in philosophy.

The difference of "women philosophers" is only a difference of repetition. It's certainly not a matter of inability; it's the lack of theoretical possibilities. All the "philosophical" topics are and always will be borrowed topics for women. The questions are and always will be given to them.

We have to admit that even the deconstruction of philosophy, which grants such an important place to gender difference and denounces the "phallogocentrism" of tradition, offers no other philosophical future to women than that of playing the replica.

Woman's possibility, philosophy's impossibility

Jacques Derrida's analysis of women's studies supports this interpretation. Don't you think that women's studies would allow women to accomplish what philosophy prohibits them from doing? Doesn't women's studies offer the possibility of opening a space up for the specificity of feminine thought and writing? Derrida is hesitant about how to answer this, questioning the specifically feminine power of intervention of women's studies.[4] Noting the tardy addition of this field of study to the traditional university model ("women's studies" is hardly forty years old today), Derrida interrogates its status: what does it change in the exercise of intellectual power? What does it allow us to displace within the institution? The immediate response is, "As much as women's studies has not put back into question the very principles of the structure of the former model of the university, it risks to be just another cell in the university beehive."[5] As Naomi Schor explains,

> Derrida goes on strongly to suggest that in the accumulation of empirical research on women, in the tenuring of feminist scholars, in the seemingly spectacular success of women's studies, the feminist critique of the institution has been scanted. In the eyes of deconstruction women's studies *is* perilously close to becoming "just another cell in the academic beehive."[6]
>
> Why? Derrida answers,

This is a question of the Law: are those involved in women's studies – teachers, students, researchers – the guardians of the Law or not? You will remember that in the parable of the Law of Kafka, between the guardian of the Law and the man from the country there is no *essential* difference: they are in oppositional but symmetric positions. We are all, as members of a university, guardians of the Law [. . .] Does that situation repeat itself for women's studies or not? Is there in the abstract or even topical idea of women's studies something which potentially has the force, if it is possible, to deconstruct the fundamental institutional structure of the university, of the Law of the university?[7]

This passage clearly demonstrates one of the major ambiguities of anti-essentialism: how do you establish an *essential* difference between women's studies and other fields of research, how do you define an *essential* identity for the political attitude of women within the institution, how do you maintain an *essential* distinction between the male and female guardians of the Law if "woman" or "women" have no essence? How do you achieve this if it is impossible to essentialize differences? Despite their intersection, the conflictual relationship between deconstructive anti-essentialism and theory (gender studies, queer studies, women's studies) and anti-essentialism is evident. Anti-essentialism destroys any claims by theory to displace the traditional limits of theory, to exist as a space of the feminine, to separate from the beehive, to be anything other than another cell in the honeycomb.

This gives rise to the fundamental question of authority. Can women exercise authority without mimicking the attitude of guardians?

I remember the shock of reading another text by Derrida on this question. It was his commentary on one of the photographs in Frederic Brenner's extraordinary book, *Diaspora*. The book is a collection of snapshots taken all over the world of Jewish women and men of all levels of society, nationalities, and cultures. One photograph that is particularly striking is of young American women rabbis "just like the men," wearing the clothing or ritualistic signs, the tallit and tefillin they are forbidden to wear. The photograph is titled "Faculty, students, rabbis, and cantors, Jewish Theological Seminary of America, New York." Derrida writes,

Theater of the *impossible*, farce or provocation, limit of identification: I have never in my life seen women wearing talliot and tefillin [. . .]. They are right to make their demands, but, as always when feminism begins, they seem to want to resemble. They mime, they identify with patriarchal authority. As a result, they are at once, depending on the case, more *and* less seductive: other limits of identification.[8]

So feminine authority looks like a mime. While the photograph creates the event of feminine authority, in doing so it immediately devalues it by marking this event with the seal of pastiche. Derrida uses "begins" after feminism ("as always when feminism begins"), but isn't it just not to be too injurious, isn't this word "begins" detachable? Isn't it the lot of all feminism, beginning or not, to "want to resemble"? Elsewhere Derrida writes, "Do not forget the daughters do not wear a tallith. The daughters, the women, the mothers, the sisters cannot and must not. They have no right to it."[9]

When I, "the woman philosopher," read these lines I felt like these women rabbis, exactly the way they are seen by Derrida, donning my concepts as if they were their cloths, shawls, or straps, with the sudden impression of playing my life out on a crazed stage, acting in both Hegel's *Science of Logic* and Woody Allen's films.

No doubt reading this passage by Derrida awoke and confirmed the certitude that talking about a woman philosopher would always be nothing but a reply to patriarchal authority, a miming of male mastery, a manner of speaking and acting to which "woman" could bring nothing "proper."

Coming from Derrida, I immediately felt this confirmation of a condemnation to imitation all the more violently because deconstruction accuses traditional metaphysics of having never recognized the specificity of the feminine. Here was my mentor, or "counter-mentor," Jacques Derrida, he who had followed my work for so many years, one of the first philosophers to give due attention to the question of the feminine in philosophy, characterizing metaphysics as a phallocentrism or phallogocentrism and showing that women's speech was another speech, one that could both offer and challenge metaphysics with a radical outside, the chance for a new way of being and writing. Moreover, this other speech is not necessarily the speech *of* a woman, but can also be the echo, in a philosopher, of another tongue, one different from the "masculine." Derrida showed us how to hear this tongue in the work of women (Gertrude Stein, Hélène Cixous . . .) as well as in Rousseau, Nietzsche, Levinas, and in his own speech. "I, myself, as a woman," he used to say, half-joking, in his seminar . . . But at the same time, who could deny that deconstruction is also a total threat for feminism, in as much as it constructs the feminine subject by killing her?

Working with Derrida as my supervisor, I was doomed to mimic a double mastery. First, the mastery of the classical philosopher – a species to which he unequivocally belonged as a former student of the *École normale supérieure*, now authoritarian tutor in this same institution, with all his famed conceptual mastery, intelligence, rigor, liveliness, quick wits, and metaphysical agility. Second, the mastery of another way of being or posture, the mastery of a feminine or feminist Derrida, attached to the deconstruction of mastery itself, determined to stigmatize and relentlessly critique the distressing comments about women and the female condition by traditional philosophers – not one escaped him. I also had to mimic the troubled thinker from an unknown land and who better than he, who other than he, was able to go so far with this? It was he who drew attention to the voices of women, thinking through the plurality of voices as the privileged echo of sexual difference. Remember these words in *Choreographies*:

> I would like to believe in the multiplicity of sexually marked voices. I would like to believe in the masses, this indeterminable number of blended voices, this mobile of non-identified sexual marks whose choreography can carry, divide, multiply the body of each "individual," whether he be classified as "man" or as "woman" according to the criteria of usage.[10]

How could I not suffer from the violence of this double mimicry? How could I bear for a man, even speaking in the name of women, "as" a woman, to speak better than they could, for them, stronger and louder than them, their conceptual and political rights? How could I bear for him to recognize with sharper acuity, sometimes with greater critical insight than they, their overexposure to violence? This ambiguity in Derrida's feminist speech is difficult to think and to live in as much as it liberates the feminine while depriving it of the authority of its own emancipation. In any case, the women and men who knew Derrida know all about his ambivalence in regard to women. Respect and fraternity, or sorority, went hand in hand with machismo, seduction, and sexual parade.

The dual constraint of this mimicry (philosophy and deconstruction) led me to understand that in the end there was nothing for a woman to conquer beyond simulacra, since simulacra is the ontological place that is always resolutely imposed on women. In the discourse of philosophy – in both metaphysics *and* deconstruction – nothing can offer itself authentically to be transformed by a woman, however stratified and multiple it may be.

Of course, this impossibility can be experienced as a liberating impossibility. The fact that there is no "authentically" feminine woman's philosophy no doubt makes it also possible to put into question the supposed substantiality of the masculine, to de-essentialize philosophy, to fluidify in a single movement sexual gender and genres of discourse.

But we are still stuck with the question of the modes of resistance to this violence awaiting women both at the entrance and the exit of metaphysics, along with the simultaneous resistance to anti-essentialist violence. How, *in her own name* and with authority, can she inscribe the philosophical impossibility of being a woman philosopher? How does she inscribe the theoretical impossibility of being a woman *in the feminine*? Emancipatory transcendence (to use Simone de Beauvoir's powerful expression) certainly did not die with either deconstruction or gender studies. The "woman" subject, in her ontological escheat, nevertheless still wants to free herself. Must she, despite everything, always remain running behind, resigning herself, pretending, inhibiting her energy, installing herself in mimicry, forever enveloping herself in tallits that are not made for her?

The plasticity of philosophy and the plasticity of "woman" must be put to the test together with this question. In what sense, and how far, can philosophy transform itself under the impact of women's resistance? In what sense can this transformation appear to be a historical evolution? In what sense is this evolution a revolution, plasticizing philosophy and constructing something completely other? Something that no longer sets woman up as a replica?

We can now consider the second meaning of the phrase "there is no woman philosopher," the militant meaning: woman transgresses the limits of philosophical space because it is inadequate for her "essence." To transgress the limits of philosophy and its violence – both metaphysical and deconstructive – does not necessarily imply giving up on concepts. Why should it? As I wrote elsewhere, concepts are never guilty; it is not concepts that carry the burden of phallogocentrism.[11] The ideology at work in concepts does not come from the concepts themselves, but from the metamorphosis of their pragmatic and motor value as noemes. As motor schemes, concepts are originally precipitates or beginnings of action, accelerators that allow us to advance, the equivalents of racing for thought. Before concepts become fixed as noemes we must find a way of creating a trans-philosophical space, one in which women are allowed to transform their impossibility of being into a specific power. And whether it is through evolution or revolution, deformation or explosion, this space can no longer be the space of philosophy; it must be philosophy impeded.

It may be that woman does not invent philosophical questions, but she certainly does create problems. She puts a spoke in the wheels of philosophers and philosophical categories wherever she can. The impossibility of being a woman thus becomes the impossibility of philosophy.

How do we move from one impossibility to the other? How do we think this change? To answer these questions, we must consider the issue of the philosophical training of women. It seems to me that at least in France women usually experience three main moments, which I'll refer to with three descriptors: *acting as if, acting together*, and *acting without*. The first refers to the training years. The second marks the discovery of feminism and its theoretical value, from the various analyses or discussions which the question of the feminine has received from women. This moment comes second because in France no woman theorist appears in the title of any program of philosophical study whatsoever, in either secondary or further education. It was therefore only very late that I discovered French authors such as Irigaray, Kristeva, and Wittig. This second moment corresponds to a new awareness of the sexed or "gendered" nature of the philosophizing and philosophical subjectivity. The distortion between the subject of philosophical statements, which are always masculine, and the female subject reading them suddenly becomes striking in itself. The woman then discovers that she belongs to another group than the "philosophers" who spontaneously understand themselves as "universal" subjects. She then begins to read the work of women who have thought through the relations between women and philosophy, all that body of work that had been so carefully hidden during her years of training. She feels her proximity and distance from these new interlocutors. Then at last comes the time when she goes off on her own, when she "acts without," abandoning all her previous encounters in order to begin to speak and to set herself up in an entirely new territory, the outline of another body, another essence. This is where she feels hope – perhaps delusional – beyond essentialism and anti-essentialism, a new idea of the feminine that starts from her own philosophical impossibility.

Acting as if

"The woman first finds herself in a state of inferiority during her period of apprenticeship," writes Beauvoir.[12] She continues,

> I remember a female student doing the *agrégation* who said, at the time when there was a coed competitive exam in philosophy: "Boys can succeed in one or two years; we need at least four." Another – who was recommended a book on Kant, a writer on the curriculum – commented "This book is too difficult: it's for Normalians!" She seemed to think that women could take easier exams; beaten before even trying, she was in effect giving all chances of success to the men.[13]

I, too, have known this timidity. I recognize this hesitation. I experienced the acerbic and misogynistic comments of my *khâgne* entrance exam philosophy professor at the prestigious Lycée Henri IV. "Now this," he would sometimes say when he was discussing something "difficult" (ah! difficulty, in philosophy! now there's a capital mystification that turns concepts into ideological bullets), "my dear young ladies, no need for you to listen to this. The ladies may think about something else." Implication: your competitive exam is easier (at that time the competitive exams were not mixed; there was one for girls – Sèvres or

Fontenay – and one for boys – Ulm or Saint-Cloud). The list of remarks of this type, scornful comments, or conversely, the open and unbearable flattery of misplaced gestures or attempts at seduction, would be too long to catalogue. Sadly, many women know them all too well.

During my years of apprenticeship, I swore that I would wring the neck of "difficult philosophy." That was my answer, for what it's worth. (And, dear sisters, I tell you now in confidence that even today I enjoy the satisfaction and secret joy of having "become just as strong as them" during this time and of having very soon lost all fear of anyone in philosophy. I'll take them all on in the ring, I said to myself, bring them on! No problem! Come on over and we'll talk about whatever you like: disjunctive syllogism? Immanent deduction in the *Doctrine of the Concept*? The question of the essence of truth in Heidegger?). In choosing to write my doctoral dissertation on Hegel and devoting myself entirely to "pure" philosophy (no aesthetics, no applied philosophy), I swore that I would build myself razor-sharp conceptual blades and lances, that my reasoning and deductions would be exemplary in their solidity, that I would be, yes it's true, *just like* the strongest man. Throw in a dose of indomitable independence, a total incapacity to entertain flattery, a deep distaste for social chitchat, an ability to detect theoretical mediocrity instantly, and an unabashed streak of savagery and you have my profile, the profile of someone who'll never have a traditional, stellar career, but (and I'm still very proud of this too) one who, *just as* Rousseau confided, has never been told what to do by anyone.

This paradoxical freedom of "acting as if" was conquered at the cost of the prohibition on narration and an insistence on the "transparency" of the author. I had to stop behaving "like a literature person," like a woman, I had to stop telling stories, I had to be no one in particular, I had to erase my "I," my gender, my character, my history, my story. I had to use that awful neuter, asexual language you find in dissertations and theses. I had to write in the style of those introductions to papers or dissertations on the works of great thinkers written by administrators. As Irigaray says quite rightly, "because women have no language sexed as female," they use a language that is "a so-called neuter language where in fact they are deprived of speech." They are not at home in this language; they do not have the "words that would allow them both to get out of and to return to their homes. To 'take off' from their bodies, give themselves a territory, an environment and invite the other to some possible share or passage."[14]

No doubt my encounter with deconstruction was born largely of the desire to rediscover what I had sacrificed, which was perhaps, quite simply, my femininity. For a long time, moreover, I assimilated writing, as described by Derrida, to woman. Even if I know that this assimilation was ultimately illegitimate, it harbors a certain truth. How can anyone deny that the accursed aspect of language – writing, repressed by centuries of metaphysics, the *a* of *différance*, in its inaudible discretion – is like woman, she who is excluded from all systems and all ontologies, shares in her invisibility, her anonymity, but also her strength, her improbable but true value as origin and place of birth?

I was acutely sensitive to the feminine in the trace, whose fragility I first saw in Levinas:

> The trace *qua* trace does not simply lead to the past, but is the very *passing* toward a past more remote than any past and any future which still are set in my time – the past of the other, in which eternity takes form, an absolute past which unites all times.[15]

This "passing" or "trace of a passage" always reminded me of Jensen's Gradiva and of a certain approach, a way of walking, the passage through which we may pass, come, and go. I could never fully avoid associating woman with the trace.

Like Hanold in Freud's text, I started to look for the woman, to look for myself, in the traces of a woman who might have affected philosophy. Derrida quite rightly emphasizes the density of so mysterious an archeology:

Woman's possibility, philosophy's impossibility

Hanold [. . .] dreams of [. . .] reliving the singular pressure or impression which Gradiva's step [*pas*], the step itself, the step of Gradiva herself, that very day, at that time, on that date, in what was inimitable about it, must have left in the ashes. He dreams this irreplaceable place, the very ash, where the singular imprint, like a signature, barely distinguishes itself from the impression. And this is the condition of singularity, the idiom, the secret, testimony. It is the condition for the uniqueness of the printer-printed, of the impression and the imprint, of the pressure and its trace in the unique *instant* where they are not yet distinguished the one from the other, forming in an *instant* a single body of Gradiva's step, of her gait, of her pace [. . .] and of the ground which carries them. The trace no longer distinguishes itself from its substrate [. . .] It must be resuscitated right where, in an absolutely safe location, in an irreplaceable place, it still holds, right on the ash, not yet having detached itself, the pressure of Gradiva's so singular step.[16]

Here, you see, femininity becomes inimitable, unique, singular. Like the trace, woman would be indiscernible, rendering the difference between form and matter invisible. The relation between the stamp and its support becomes imperceptible, ungraspable by mimesis or by the replica of authority. If, as Montaigne says, man can accompany himself

117

everywhere, then perhaps woman can displace everything, without saying a thing and without showing
anything, she with a body that carries the ground on
which she walks, a ground that is as dark and crum-
bling as ash, the secret grounds of all discourse. In
that way she would secretly ensure, as she walks, the
movement of the supposedly immutable foundation
of metaphysics, threatening it with a slight tremor and
suggesting the mysteries of an obscure tectonics, the
roots of the Cartesian tree.

Woman also appears as one of the privileged
figures of writing, fusing print and support and
even the erasure of this fusion, the excluded
instance in its value of *archè*. Recognizing this
archeology and returning rights to the femininity
that had been flouted, deconstruction put an end
to the reign of the philosophical text as a prison
house of language, censor of image and literature.
There is plenty to say about how Derrida inscribed
woman in the text, style, tone, and approach, as
well as in the subjects of thought. No philosopher
went as far as he in this sharing of roles and mixing
of voices.

But, as I said earlier, eventually I had to recognize that deconstruction did not offer women any
real freedom to create. What "woman philosopher"
could invent from deconstruction? If she wanted to
survive, didn't she have to side-step, take another
path, lift her foot up from the print left in the

ashes to go off on her own, alone, exposed, but free? You could of course ask the "men" these same questions (Has anyone ever invented anything whatsoever in deconstruction after Derrida? Has anyone done anything other than mummify, worship, turn to stone the figure of the master? Has anyone ever escaped the involuntary pastiche which Proust described as being "condemned to live forever attached to the tongue of a bell?"[17]). But these questions are still all the more acute for women who, after their awakening, their exit from metaphysical silence, and their impossibility as philosophical subjects, *ought to have taken their turn*, inventing a speech, opening a space beyond-metaphysics, ensuring the future.

Yet how could they have done this, since the "feminine" is caught in the system through a dual constraint: it appears as an ontological promise (as a mode of being always repressed by philosophy and therefore as a mode of being that is always to come), while at the same time it is nothing but a new figure of the "proper"? The difficulties that I presented in "The Meaning of the 'Feminine'" emphasize the impossible possibility of the feminine in and for deconstruction.

I experienced this impossibility personally in the critique Derrida gave my concept of plasticity in "A Time for Farewells . . ."[18] It's a very beautiful, subtle critique that starts off with words of praise: the bringing to light of plasticity can only be the work of a *"plastiqueuse,"* that is, an *explosive plastic artist.* So I was well and truly granted the role of creator. At the same time, as I show in "The phoenix, the spider, and the salamander," Derrida constantly insists on the fact that because of the pregnancy of plasticity, because of the motif of form in plasticity, the concept draws a very traditional relation to the future as "to see (what is) coming," anticipation, dampening the surprise. And so, in fact, the fuse of my explosive peters out, my explosive plasticity is impossible. To say "form" is actually to say "essence," in other words, yet again, "presence," the proof of substantial proximity. By refusing plasticity and its attachment to essence, deconstruction remains inviolable for Derrida; it cannot be subject to plastic explosives and is not plastifiable, it keeps on going as if nothing had ever changed.

My own need to escape from the constant escape of deconstruction took the form of a reconsideration of the mobility of the trace, the role of writing, that inexhaustible racy racer in Derrida's work. The identity of woman and writing that I had always posited eventually became suspicious in my eyes. Writing, with its displacement and *faux-bond*, never stops. In this sense, writing is not really exposed, it is not fragile enough. To elude "essence," the trace makes itself tireless, always elsewhere, always rebelling against its capture, always other. But as a result of this "always," since it denies all plasticity, writing never grows old, writing never changes.

The possibility of detecting, in writing itself or behind it, another rhythm, another economy than its own, the possibility of allowing for a different understanding of essence – essence as change and metamorphosis – led me, as I explain here in "Grammatology and plasticity," to imagine the arrival of a supplementary change, that is, of a *change of difference*. The arrival of a more modifiable structure than that of writing, one that is destined to the deforming and reforming of forms without being attached to an initial evidence, a presence or first form. One that would also be without eternal youth, without this always fresh and untouched resistance of writing and *différance*.

The tangled design and form of neuronal connections offer a schema for this coral-like redefinition of a movement that secretly saps the health of the trace by marking arrests, the plastic folds in its progress. You could say that plasticity is the body of the trace. And this makes the trace impossible. In this sense it is "women's" work.

The "feminine" would then perhaps be that which, even within writing, carves out another body than that of writing, a body that refuses to allow itself to be erased by the very erasability of the trace, the trace that never has even the tiniest wrinkle. Plasticity renders impossible the inconvertibility of the trace into anything other than itself and ruins any claim to resist transformation.

Acting together

But to return to my initial question, how, despite everything, do you inscribe this new understanding of essence without offering yourself up, once again, to the deconstructive knife?

This leads to the fundamental question: can woman find her place? Doesn't her place always come from the other; isn't it always given to her by the other? These questions eventually led the philosopher to read other "women," engaged in the term "woman philosopher." To think *with* them. Can woman find her home? This question resonates strongly in the writing of Irigaray, who, in my eyes, is by far the most convincing and most daring "'feminist' woman philosopher." A time comes when you turn to texts that seek to situate the feminine in philosophy, as its non-place, in texts by women that you often discover through the detour of the United States, away from home, escaping. It is time to take on a lesbian becoming of thought that seems to be the only remedy to the violence to women.

Discussing the non-place of woman, caught between home and work life, between femininity and maternity, Irigaray writes, "The maternal-feminine remains the *place separated from 'its' own place*, deprived of 'its' place. She is, or ceaselessly becomes, the place of the other who cannot separate himself from it. Without her knowing or willing it, she is then threatening because of what she lacks: a 'proper' place." In order for such a place to exist, there would have to be a "change in the whole economy of space-time."[19]

For Irigaray this "change in space-time" occurs through an *active* engagement with mimicry or simulacra that turns them into strategies. Woman is no longer the victim of mime; she becomes its subversive instance. For women it is a matter of accepting the posture of simulation of masculine discourse by producing its subversive repetition, a copy of the copy in order to succeed in transforming mime into a voluntary and liberating pastiche. In *This Sex Which Is Not One*, Irigaray writes,

> One must assume the feminine role deliberately. Which means already to convert a form of subordination into an affirmation and thus to begin to thwart it. [. . .] To play with mimesis is thus, for a woman, to try to recover the place of her exploitation by discourse, without allowing herself to be simply reduced to it. It means to resubmit herself — inasmuch as she is on the side of the "perceptible," of "matter" — to "ideas," in particular to ideas about herself, that are elaborated in/by a masculine logic,

but so as to make "visible," by an effect of playful repetition, what was supposed to remain invisible: the cover-up of a possible operation of the feminine in language. It also means "to unveil" the fact that, if women are such good mimics, it is because they are not simply resorbed in this function. *They also remain elsewhere* [. . .].[20]

The "sex" assigned to woman on the pretext of thinking the category of the feminine in a traditional manner becomes unrepresentable in the discourse that mobilizes this category since the feminine is non-universal and thus without any real status as a subject. This is why Irigaray can write that woman is "this sex that is not one." Strategic mimicry involves making visible the exclusion of the feminine from discourse – particularly from philosophical discourse – as well as from the corpus of philosophy, inventing a type of reading able to render the exclusion manifest. Speaking like "male" philosophers, but utilizing their concepts in such a way as to turn them not towards what they say but towards what they don't say (the feminine), it is possible to create an arena for speech where that which is ignored appears as a negative.

To mimic thus involves revisiting the metaphysics of substance "in the style of," each time emphasizing the matter/form couple presupposed by this metaphysics. Irigaray demonstrates that the feminine does not in fact appear, as one might think, as matter opposed to "masculine" form; rather the feminine presents as the *other* of the matter/form couple, as this *other materiality* rejected by the matter/form couple, the *matter of matter* if you like. Woman, in philosophical space, is the matter that no other matter waiting for form can either touch or move, a matter limited to itself – "a vessel." "The female sex (organ) is neither matter nor form but *vessel*," writes Irigaray in *An Ethics of Sexual Difference*, playing on the two meanings in French of the word "*vase*," which means both a molded form and mud.[21] This excluded materiality is exposed, for instance, in the superb mimetic reading of *Timaeus* Irigaray gives in *Speculum*.[22] The excluded materiality of the woman appears there in the *khôra* (a receptacle that "receives all bodies" (*ta panta somata*) (50 b)), a materiality that is both motherly and the impossibility of the feminine, present and absent in the text, an ontologically stateless materiality, one without which philosophical discourse would not be able to function.

The "essence" of woman is thus neither matter nor form; it is achieved beyond traditional ontological and metaphysical determinations, outside pairs of conceptual opposites, in an exterior destined to exile and erasure. None of the images, none of the figures, none of the metaphors of the philosophical tradition correspond to woman. For this reason, the ontological and tropical impossibility of the figure of the *khôra* becomes the figure without a figure of woman, her "essence" read in filigree.

In *Bodies that Matter*, Butler analyzes this mimetic strategy in an illuminating manner:

> Irigaray mimes *mimesis* itself. Through miming, Irigaray transgresses the prohibition against resemblance at the same time that she refuses the notion of resemblance as copy. She cites Plato again and again, but the citations expose precisely what is excluded from them and seek to show and to reintroduce the excluded into the system itself. In this sense, she performs a repetition and displacement of the phallic economy. *This is citation, not as enslavement or simple reiteration of the original, but as an insubordination that appears to take place within the very terms of the original and which calls into question the power of origination that Plato appears to claim for himself.* [. . .] This textual practice is not grounded in a rival ontology, but inhabits – indeed, penetrates, occupies and redeploys – the paternal language itself.[23]

Patriarchal authority is subverted and reinvested by that which displaces it. It is a matter of undoing misogynistic discourse through the effect of parodic repetition, revealing the feminine in a way that is unfamiliar, in its uncanniness, you could say. But Butler attacks the ambiguity of this discourse: to assume that "the feminine belongs to women," she writes, is an "assumption surely suspect."[24] Furthermore, to mime philosophy is also to mime the errors of philosophy.[25] Despite the displacement and discrepancy, in Irigaray we find the same tone, the same ambition, the same seriousness, the same philosophical drive as in traditional authors. Once again the attempt to theorize the feminine becomes subject to essentialist suspicion. As my previous analyses of the status of lips showed, any attempt to schematize (in the sense of figuration) feminine specificity is immediately suspect.

From the point of view of the anti-essentialists things are no better if we turn to another very important aspect of Irigaray's work in which she has sought, beyond or alongside her mimetic gesture, to define a mechanics of female sexuality through science, particularly physics. More specifically, the mechanism of fluids takes female sexuality into account, unbeknown to scientists who have never produced a "theory of fluids" from the mechanics of fluids. Science, which Irigaray distrusts just as much as she distrusts philosophy in so far as it excludes the feminine (the scientific subject is never sexed or gendered), has not developed a theory of the kind of economy of liquidity, a theory able to characterize the ways of being or phenomena which would most appropriately be called femininity. Science never loses it; science never transforms itself into anything other than a series of "neutral" statements about supposedly asexual objects ("universals" once again).

Yet fluids are connected to the *jouissance* of fluids,

their body and consistency: "it seems to me that the pleasure of the fluid subsists, in women, far beyond the so-called oral stage: the pleasure of "what's flowing" within her, outside of her and indeed among women."[26] The properties of fluids, which are all linked to being "mobile, uncertain,"[27] allow us to identify a form of the ontological primacy of the feminine starting with the ontological primacy of fluids and liquids themselves (the Heraclitean "everything flows" and its original value). Fluid is no longer a "metaphor," it is the material assumption of woman's real; woman who is excluded from the matter/form relation precisely as a fluid. This is why, as Naomi Schor explains, "The real in Irigaray is neither impossible, nor unknowable: it is the fluid. [. . .] Irigaray insistently associates the fluid and the real, speaking of 'the real of the dynamic of fluids' and 'an economy of *real fluids*'."[28] "Is there no fluidity, no deluge that could shake up the social order?" Irigaray asks.[29] Fluidity, which is clearly associated with lips, appears as that which simultaneously escapes, is excluded and flees this exclusion, managing to upset the order, opposing the liquid evanescence of another source to patriarchal authority in all its solidity. To return to the "acting together" that characterizes this second moment in the process of women's philosophical training, I wonder, however, whether ultimately, following the course of this river, flowing with its lips, borrowing this secret mouth to speak, feminine can amount to a viable theoretical approach. Irigaray was accused of both ontological and biological essentialism. I do not agree with these accusations, which I find largely petty and irrelevant; my problem is of another sort: to act as if, to follow philosophical mime as Irigaray suggests we do, strikes me as impossible not on account of the risk of essentialism, but because of the danger of getting stuck in repetition.

Ultimately, we find ourselves caught in the cycle of a writing and analysis that always say the same thing in the end, sometimes until it becomes entirely sterile. Let's take the example of the reading of Spinoza developed in *An Ethics of Sexual Difference*. Commenting on the first propositions of his *Ethics*, Irigaray declares:

> Here Spinoza is talking about God. Only God is in himself, conceived by himself; needing the concept of no other thing in order to be formed. Only God generates his existence out of his essence; which means also that he engenders himself in the form of concepts without having need of concepts different from himself in order to be formed.[30]

For Irigaray this definition of God is purely and simply a definition of the masculine. Indeed,

> It also seems that *Man* conceives himself without anyone else, except God, forming his conception.

129

[. . .] This would not be the case for *woman*, who would correspond to no conception. Who, as the Greeks saw it, lacks fixed form and idea and lacks above all a conception that she provides for herself. As matter, or extension for the concept, she would have no conception at her disposal, would be unable to conceive herself or conceive the other and, theoretically, she would need to pass through man in order to have a relation, for herself, to man, to the world and to God. If indeed she is capable of any of this.[31]

Aside from the fact that this reading is not illuminating and misses the real ontological difficulty of the *Ethics*, the arguments employed are always the same, repeating what was already said about *Timaeus*. Woman is the place without a place of a materiality which is not passive materiality, which can always take form, auto-engender, and develop itself. Woman eludes form. And so she remains "pure disposable 'matter.' Pure receptacle that does not stay still. Not even a place, then?"[32] She always stands apart from the divine, outside God, if you will.

This analysis could go on and on, serving as a key for reading all philosophical doctrines. But what's the point? How do you leave the iterability of feminine thought as an obstacle to the concept, how do you escape the infinite fluidity or elasticity of woman's matter?

As we have seen, Irigaray opposes a bodily posture of mimicry, simulacra, and disguise to her understanding of the feminine as the residual matter of philosophical discourse. Defining woman as the excluded one of philosophical categories, Irigaray presents a knowledge of woman that is negatively defined as exclusion, outside the field of knowledge. Yet it seems that to play with simulacra, to think exclusion does not offer much to the question of the possibility of a philosophy "of" woman, it gives it no "place." It will always be possible to identify the hollow left by the absence of the feminine in the negative, in a traditional philosophical doctrine. To do so systematically nullifies the critical weight, just as the deconstruction of presence ultimately takes place but no longer says anything at all. The problem with strategic mimicry is that it, too, can be subject to mime or pastiche. It therefore loses its subversive value. The "woman philosopher," if for the sake of argument we allow for the existence of this conceptual monster, finds no future in the constant identification of its "material absence" from works. The offensive feminine mime *is itself struck down by its own impossibility*.

Butler analyses the problem of inevitable repetition in Irigaray and proposes another way of approaching texts. All matrices of textual intelligibility establish (and are established by) gender norms that make it impossible to separate the intellectual understanding

---

of the text from the materialization of a body in that text. Philosophical understanding always reveals, usually unbeknown to it, first, what concept of the body is at work in the text and, second, how the body of the male or female reader responds, echoes or resists this concept.

For example, in *The Psychic Life of Power*, Butler interprets the master/slave relation in Hegel as a gesture of denegation of the body: the master asks the slave to be "his body for him" (*You Be My Body For Me!*).[33] Butler shows that the body is the object of constant disavowal in Hegel. No doubt this observation could be extended to philosophers other than Hegel and the figure of the denial of the body could be constituted as a paradigm or operative schema for reading philosophical texts in general. For the interpreter it would be a matter of stating the meaning of this denial, the normative matrix that underlies it, and the ways of displacing or subverting it. This new hermetic strategy thus assumes plasticity in the gender of the reader, who must not impose the series of norms she is criticizing in the text she is reading. In *Gender Trouble*, Butler shows that "in recent years, however, that theory, or set of theories, has migrated into gender and sexuality studies, postcolonial and race studies."[34] The common axiom in both of these types of studies, which exceed "feminism," is the exercising of a constant vigilance regarding the reader's gender identity. The suppleness and mobility of this identity are required in order to foil, whenever possible, the triple assignation of the reader, the subject of the enunciation, and the subject of the statement to normative residences. It is less a matter of contesting a pre-established value system through mimicry (by identifying the place of exclusion) than of knowing how not to repeat this system when identifying the exclusion.

Once again, according to Butler, involuntary repetition is often the fate of "feminist philosophers." But it is not for all that a matter of abandoning the mimicry strategy; rather the practice is radicalized, extended into transvestitism. *Gender Trouble* opens a politico-hermeneutic space in which sexual transvestitism (drag, transgender . . .) intersects with noetic transvestitism: the identity of the interpreter is displaced by his or her reading, it is not fixed, it transforms itself according to the text. The concept of the performativity of gender allows Butler to posit simultaneously the non-substantiality of sexual gender (there is no ontological reality or perhaps any biological masculine or feminine as such) and of the reading or writing subjects.

Performativity means that gender is acted out through a series of permanent and always parodic rituals that evoke transvestitism and another new form of imitation, one which is perhaps irreducible to mimicry or *mimesis*.

———

133

In imitating gender, drag implicitly reveals the imitative structure of gender itself – as well as its contingency. Indeed, part of the pleasure, the giddiness of the performance is in the recognition of a radical contingency in the relation between sex and gender in the face of cultural configurations of causal unities that are regularly assumed to be natural and necessary. In the place of the law of heterosexual coherence, we see sex and gender denaturalized by means of a performance which avows their distinctness and dramatizes the cultural mechanism of their fabricated unity.

The notion of gender parody defended here does not assume that there is an original which such parodic identities imitate. Indeed, the parody is *of* the very notion of an original, [. . .] gender parody reveals that the original identity after which gender fashions itself is an imitation without an origin. To be more precise, it is a production which, in effect – that is, in its effects – *postures as an imitation.*[35]

To interpret a text starting from this sort of performance praxis would thus amount to deconstituting the neutrality of the subject of the enunciated as well as the subject of the enunciation by showing how, within the supposed universality of philosophical propositions, the body is denied, displaced, but never annihilated. The philosophical subject would always be the one who asks the other, will "you be my body for me?" This denied transvestitism of the body must be repeated by an active transvestitism, transforming itself into the body of the author for a while. "Acting together" would perhaps be to enter into the market of this symbolic exchange, to co-author, for example, to no longer imitate authority but rather to multiply its masks, playing Duck, Duck, Goose with bodies, to pass among them. In short, acting together is another way of making philosophy impossible.

Acting without

For all that a transvestite approach is fascinating, it leaves the idea of the feminine somewhat behind, even if this idea is always present in Butler's work. Personally, I have discovered that it is totally impossible for me to give up the schema "woman." I cannot succeed in dissolving it into the schema of gender or "queer multitudes." I continue to see myself as a woman. I know very well that this word is plastic, that it cannot be constituted as a separate reality, and that, as I wrote in "The Meaning of the 'Feminine,'" "there is no reason to privilege the 'feminine,' or to name the crossroads of ontic-ontological exchange 'feminine,'" I know that the feminine is one of the "passing, metabolic points of identity."

Still, I believe that *the word "woman" has a meaning outside the heterosexual matrix*. It is tedious to keep bringing it back there, making it the site of a constant parody, and it no longer offers me anything "philosophically." I'm also aware that there's good reason not to hang onto it as you would a thing – but I have shown, after all, the plasticity of things by emphasizing the strong metamorphic tenor with which they are ontologically invested.

"Essence": there has always been a misunderstanding of this term which, as Heidegger shows (and I have emphasized this point), has only ever designated, under the skin of metaphysics and despite ontological dogma, the transformability of beings, never their substantial stability. In the end essence does not say presence; it says *entry* into presence, in other words, an originary movement that, again, is the movement of change or exchange. Hegel knew this already, playing on the German words *Wesen* and *Gewesen* in *Science of Logic*, where he states that "essence is past [. . .] Being," its memory, that is, it is also something that it is no longer entirely and that measures the space of a transformation that Hegel thinks, rightly or wrongly, as the dialectical work that never leaves identity in peace.[36] The accusation of "essentialism" only means something at the price of a total philosophical ignorance of the meaning of the word "essence." The debate between essentialism and anti-essentialism is based on a current, ordinary conception of essence. And at this point in the argument don't tell me that I hide behind the "authority" of Hegel or Heidegger too often. I've worked hard in my own way to make their lives impossible too.

The concept of "form" cannot be reduced to the evidence of presence either. Consequently, as I showed in "Grammatology and plasticity," plasticity calls for the transgression of presence, a transgression that is always understood in essence and thus in form, in things. *Plastiqueuse.* That's what Derrida called me. The plastic explosive artist here is not me; it's essence.

Anatomical essentialism? But again, why should we have it in for biology? Why think that biology is in any way responsible for a sort of determinism founded on the supposed obviousness of the form of bodies? The *biological* quarrel of essentialism and anti-essentialism has no more meaning than the *onto-logical* quarrel. The plasticity of gender does not refer to the halted evidence of a form any more than the plasticity of essence. We must rethink the relation of philosophy and science today, not in order to isolate a "feminine" continent that would be, for example, the mechanics of fluids, but rather to show, always according to the hypothesis of an originary trans-formability of presence and nature, that *the place of sex has moved.* My interest in contemporary neurobiology has led me to discover the emphasis of researchers on the emotional brain. This insistence coincides with what I interpret as the emergence of a new libidinal economy. Today the brain is becoming the place of affects, passions, and drives, delocalizing "sexuality" from the central, etiological role – both psychic and genital – with which Freud endowed it. This does not mean that gender identity is only developed by neurons, but that the space of play between (anatomic) sex and gender, between the so-called "biological essence" and "cultural construction" of identity, has profoundly changed meaning. To construct one's identity must no longer only be considered a way of occupying and dividing the space between sex and gender by multiplying the masks or processes of "deterritorialization" of the body, a deterritorialization "that forces a resistance to the processes of 'normal' becoming."[37] To construct one's identity is a process that can only be a development of an original biological malleability, a first transformability. If sex were not plastic, there would be no gender. If something were not offered for transformation in the natural and anatomical determination of sex, then identity construction would not be possible. This originary transformability is intimately connected to cerebral plasticity. The entire process of mutation by the injection or ingestion of hormones, for example, discussed by Preciado in *Testojunkie*, initially occurs in the brain. We must explore closely this connection between sex and the brain that endows both with a degree of originary suppleness without which there would in effect be a "biological essence of beings," a pure fantasy, which is no doubt hard to shake off, but only in ideology. As the current incredible growth in epigenetics proves, biology is not essentialist. The space between "bio" and "trans" is perhaps already, in itself, a biological phenomenon . . .

I am not saying that gender studies ought to prioritize the study of a possible gender difference between brains: women's brains, men's brains, etc. These studies of the gender of the brain exist and are legitimate. But they do not interest me as such. What matters to me when I insist on the cerebral dimension of gender is deconstructing the idea of biological rigidity and showing, once again, that there are no grounds for a concept of essence, conceived of as substance, be it ontological or natural. Transformability is at work from the start, it trumps all determination. Everything starts with metamorphosis.

Consequently, perhaps it is not so urgent to contest the schema of fluidity, of liquidity, of lips, if you consider that these schema do not refer to anything that is fixed, but rather help to think the impossibility of the philosophical place of woman. The very possibility of the emergence of woman as impossibility.

I have shown why Irigaray's approach might appear to fall short. We must open new paths, but we must not reject, in the name of a radical "anti-essentialism," the work that led to this *insistence* on the feminine. Once again, anti-essentialist violence and deconstructive violence work hand in hand to empty woman of herself, to disembowel her. In this sense, they match ordinary violence. Perhaps women

---

have changed nothing in institutional authority and the exercise of such authority, but then again nor has deconstruction and gender theory. After all, perhaps that's not even the problem.

There comes a time to "do without," to leave behind the masculine, the feminine, and all the other models. A time to abandon the question of authority. One only becomes an authority when one decides to mock authority. This is no doubt the last stage in training and perhaps even in life. A time comes when we know that philosophy has nothing more to offer, that it cannot welcome the fugitive essence of women, that gender studies or deconstruction cannot do so either. We must go off our own, move on, break with, clear new spaces, become possible, in other words, give up power. Power can do nothing against the possible.

No doubt woman will never become impenetrable, inviolable. That's why it is necessary to imagine the possibility of woman starting from the structural impossibility she experiences of not being violated, in herself and outside, everywhere. An impossibility that echoes the impossibility of her welcome in philosophy.

But, they'll ask me, aren't you at all a philosopher? What about the books you write, what are they worth?

Ain't I a philosopher? It's possible that I am one, but as you have seen, if I'm a philosopher it is at the price of a tremendous violence, the violence that philosophy constantly does to me and the violence I inflict on it in return. My relation to philosophy looks a lot like a constant, fierce quarrel between a man and a woman. But the outcome of this battle is ever more uncertain and unexpected. As my thinking develops I am un-marrying, de-coupling, divorcing myself a little from philosophy. I am thought absolutely, thought isolated, absolutely isolated. I cross the philosophical field in an absolute solitude. And so now there are no more limits, no more walls, nothing holds me back. It's my only chance. Perhaps something will come of this disorientation. Then I'll come back to the procession I left, the procession of the progressive march towards liberation. Women's liberation?

Notes

The meaning of the "feminine"

1 For example, the Centre d'études féminines (Center for Women's Studies) at the University of Paris-VIII was renamed the Centre d'études féminines et d'études de genre (Center for Women's and Gender Studies). What I am problematizing here is precisely the "and" that links and separates the "women" from "gender."

2 Luce Irigaray, *An Ethics of Sexual Difference*, trans. Carolyn Burke and Gillian C. Gill, Ithaca: Cornell University Press, 1993.

3 See Emmanuel Levinas, *Existence and Existents*, trans. Alphonso Lingis, Dordrecht: Kluwer Academic Publishers, 1988.

4 René Descartes, *The Passions of the Soul*, trans. Stephen Voss, Indianapolis: Hackett Publishing Company, 1989.

5 Irigaray, *Ethics of Sexual Difference*, p. 12. I recommend Marguerite La Caze's excellent article, "The

Encounter between Wonder and Generosity,"
Hypatia, 17 (3), pp. 1–13.

6 Descartes, *Passions of the Soul*, art. 53, p. 52.

7 Ibid., art. 155, p. 105.

8 Irigaray, *Ethics of Sexual Difference*, p. 75.

9 Ibid.

10 Ibid., pp. 81–82. Irigaray connects the first passion of the *Treatise*, wonder (*admiration*), to the last, generosity. Wonder is the passion of difference, while generosity is the passion of the same. But generosity is not, for all that, a reduction to the identical, since it involves seeing in the other the universality of the opening to difference: "Those who have this understanding and this feeling about themselves [generous self-esteem] are easily convinced that every other man can also have them about himself, because there is nothing therein that depends on others" (Descartes, *Passions of the Soul*, art. 154, p. 104).

11 See Irigaray, *Ethics of Sexual Difference*, p. 80.

12 In a reading of Descartes clearly influenced by Levinas, Deleuze also sees wonder as the ethical passion of difference in as much as it shows on the face, or more fundamentally, transforms a countenance into a face. As he explains, in Descartes, wonder, thought of as "astonishment that the English word *wonder* has preserved," "marks a minimum of movement for a maximum of unity, reflecting and reflected on the face"

(Gilles Deleuze, *The Movement-Image*, trans. Hugh Tomlinson and Barbara Habberjam, London: Athlone Press, 1986, p. 88). The countenance crossed with wonder is pure "affect," that is, the opening to difference "close up."

13 Jacques Derrida, *On Touching – Jean-Luc Nancy*, trans. Christine Irizarry, Stanford: Stanford University Press, 2005, p. 347, n. 5.

14 "To self-touch you" – taken from Jean-Luc Nancy's book, *Corpus* (Paris: Métailié, 1992, p. 36) – is the title of Chapter XII in Derrida, *On Touching*.

15 L. Irigaray, *Marine Lover of Friedrich Nietzsche*, trans. Gillian C. Gill, New York: Columbia University Press, pp. 91ff, cited in Derrida, *On Touching*, p. 347.

16 L. Irigaray, *Elemental Passions*, trans. Joanne Collie and Judith Still, New York: Routledge, 1992, p. 634, cited in Derrida, *On Touching*, p. 348.

17 Irigaray, *Ethics of Sexual Difference*, p. 18.

18 See in particular Derrida, *On Touching*, pp. 20–21.

19 Ibid.

20 Ibid., p. 20.

21 Ibid., p. 21.

22 See J. Derrida, "Ja, or the *faux-bond*," in *Points . . . Interviews 1974–1994*, ed. Elizabeth Weber, trans. Peggy Kamuf, Stanford: Stanford University Press, 1995, pp. 30–80.

23 J. Derrida, *Adieu – to Emmanuel Levinas*, trans.

Pascale-Anne Brault and Michael Naas, Stanford: Stanford University Press, 1999, p. 45.

24 Derrida, *Adieu*, p. 43.
25 Ibid., p. 44.
26 E. Levinas, *Totality and Infinity*, trans. Alphonso Lingis, Pittsburgh: Duquesne University Press, 1969, p. 157.
27 Derrida, *Adieu*, p. 45.
28 Levinas, *Totality and Infinity*, pp. 157–58.
29 Ibid., p. 156.
30 On this topic see the chapter on Levinas in Irigaray's *Ethics of Sexual Difference*, "The Fecundity of the Caress: A Reading of Levinas, *Totality and Infinity*, 'Phenomenology of Eros'," pp. 185ff.
31 See Judith Butler, "a feminine penetration of the feminine," *Bodies that Matter: On the Discursive Limits of Sex*, New York: Routledge, 1993, p. 51.
32 Levinas, *Totality and Infinity*, p. 156.
33 E. Levinas, "And God Created Woman," *Nine Talmudic Readings*, trans. Annette Aronowicz, Bloomington: Indiana University Press, 1990, p. 168.
34 Ibid., p. 173.
35 Ibid., p. 143.
36 Ibid., p. 177.
37 Derrida, *Adieu*, p. 44.
38 Ibid., p. 43.
39 Cited in Derrida, *On Touching*, p. 347.

40 J. Butler, *Gender Trouble*, New York: Routledge, 1990, p. 30. Published in France in a French translation by Cynthia Kraus in 2005.
41 Butler, *Gender Trouble*, p. 13.
42 Derrida, *Adieu*, p. 44.
43 Derrida, *On Touching*, p. 21. Nevertheless, in "The Laws of Reflection: Nelson Mandela, in Admiration," we find a very positive reference in Derrida to Cartesian wonder, defined as a fascination for difference, the impossibility of deciding between activity and passivity: "[Admiration] translates emotion, astonishment, surprise, interrogation in the face of that which oversteps the mark: in the face of the 'extraordinary,' says Descartes, and he considers it a passion, the first of the six primitive passions, before love, hate, desire, joy, and sadness. [. . .] The admiring look is astonished, it questions its intuition, it opens upon the light of a question but of a question received no less than asked." Derrida, in Jacques Derrida and Mustapha Tlili (eds.), *For Nelson Mandela*, New York: Seaver Books, 1987, pp. 14–15.
44 Derrida, *On Touching*, p. 21.
45 J.-L. Nancy, *The Experience of Freedom*, trans. Bridget McDonald, cited in Derrida, *On Touching*, p. 146.
46 J. Derrida, "Geschlecht, Sexual Difference, Ontological Difference," *Research in Phenomenology*, XIII, pp. 82–83.

47 Derrida, *On Touching*, p. 83.
48 Butler, *Gender Trouble*, p. 10.
49 Derrida, *On Touching*, pp. 85–86 (quotations from Levinas, *Totality and Infinity*, pp. 258–59).
50 *On Touching,* p. 87.
51 "Hypotyposis," in the Kantian sense, "consists in making a concept sensuous and is either *schematic* or *symbolic*," Immanuel Kant, *Critique of Judgment*, trans. Werner S. Pluhar, Indianapolis: Hackett Publishing, 1987, para. 59.
52 C. Malabou, *Le Change Heidegger: Du fantastique en philosophie*, Paris: Léo Scheer, 2004, published in English as *The Heidegger Change*, trans. Peter Skafish, New York: SUNY, forthcoming.
53 Malabou, *The Heidegger Change.*

Grammatology and plasticity

1 An earlier version of this chapter was published as an article, C. Malabou, "The End of Writing? Grammatology and Plasticity," trans. Annjeanette Wiese, *European Legacy*, 12 (4), 2007, pp. 431–41.
2 The Littré dictionary definition is cited in J. Derrida, *Of Grammatology*, trans. Gayatri Chakravorty Spivak, Baltimore: Johns Hopkins University Press, 1997, p. 323, n. 4.
3 With one exception that Derrida recognizes in his reference to I. J. Gelb's *A Study of Writing: The Foundations of Grammatology*, Chicago, 1952,

a book which, nonetheless, "follows the classical model of histories of writing" (Derrida, *Of
Grammatology*, p. 323.)
4 Derrida, *Of Grammatology*, p. 27.
5 Ibid., p. 93.
6 J. Derrida, *Resistances of Psychanalysis*, trans. Peggy
Kamuf, Pascale-Anne Brault, and Michael Naas,
Stanford: Stanford University Press, 1998, p. 52.
7 Ferdinand de Saussure, *Course in General Linguistics*,
trans. Wade Baskin, New York: McGraw-Hill
Books, 1959, p. 16.
8 "Even though semiology was in fact more general
and more comprehensive than linguistics, it con-
tinued to be regulated as if it were one of the
areas of linguistics. The linguistic sign remained
exemplary for semiology, it dominated it as the
master-sign and as the generative model: the
pattern [patron]" (Derrida, *Of Grammatology*,
p. 51).
9 Ibid., p. 7. As we know, the expression the "signifier of the signifier" comes from Saussure's *Course
in General Linguistics*.
10 Derrida, *Of Grammatology*, p. 30.
11 Ibid., p. 29.
12 Ibid., p. 51.
13 Ibid., p. 4.
14 Ibid., p. 74.
15 Ibid., p. 83.
16 Ibid., pp. 56–57.

17 Ibid., p. 44.
18 Ibid., p. 44.
19 See the second part of *Of Grammatology*, ch. I, "The Violence of the Letter: From Levi-Strauss to Rousseau."
20 Ibid., p. 55.
21 Ibid., p. 74 (my emphasis).
22 Cf. ibid., p. 60: "Arche-writing, movement of *différance*, irreducible arche-synthesis, opening in one and the same possibility, temporalization as well as relationship with the other and language [. . .]."
23 Ibid., pp. 6–7.
24 Ibid., p. 9.
25 François Jacob, *La Logique du vivant*, Paris: Gallimard, 1970, published in English as *The Logic of Life: A History of Heredity*, trans. Betty E. Spillmann, New York: Pantheon Books, 1974.
26 On this point, allow me to cite my book *Plasticity at the Dusk of Writing*: "All thought needs a *scheme*, that is, a *motif*, produced by a rational imagination, enabling it to force open the door to an epoch and open up exegetical perspectives suited to it" (C. Malabou, *Plasticity at the Dusk of Writing*, trans. Carolyn Shread, New York: Columbia University Press, 2010, p. 13). The "motor scheme" is the meeting point of a pure image, in other words, a concept – in this instance arche-writing or *différance* – and an existing, intuited reality – here

the pregnancy of the graphic as a code, program or inscription. Thus constituted, a motor scheme "is a type of tool capable of garnering the greatest quantity of energy and information in the text of an epoch. It gathers and develops the meanings and tendencies that impregnate the culture at a given moment as *floating images*, which constitute, both vaguely and definitely, a material 'atmosphere' or *Stimmung* ('humor,' 'affective tonality')." At the same time the motor scheme imprints the mark or brand of the concept (*Plasticity at the Dusk of Writing*, p. 14).

27 Derrida, *Of Grammatology*, p. 27.
28 On the topic of the potential of reprogramming (stem cells, RNA interference), see my article "Les régénerés. Cellules souches, thérapie génique, clonage" [Regenerated: stem cells, gene therapy, cloning], *Critique*, 709–10, special issue on "Mutants," Paris: Minuit, 2006, pp. 529–40.
29 Valentino Braitenberg, *Cortex: Statistics and Geometry of Neuronal Connectivity*, Berlin: Springer-Verlag, 1998, p. 195.
30 Ibid.
31 J. Derrida, *Writing and Difference*, trans. Alan Bass, Chicago: University of Chicago Press, p. 214.
32 Derrida, *Of Grammatology*, pp. 107–08.
33 See Malabou, *Plasticity at the Dusk of Writing*, ch. xi.
34 J. Derrida, "Différance," in Derrida, *Margins of*

Philosophy, trans. Alan Bass, Chicago: University of Chicago Press, 1982, p. 7.

The phoenix, the spider, and the salamander

1 An earlier version of this chapter was published as an article: C. Malabou, "Again: 'The wounds of the Spirit heal, and leave no scars behind'," trans. Annjeanette Wiese, *Mosaic* 40 (2), June 2007, pp. 27–37.
2 J. Derrida, "A Time for Farewells. Heidegger (read by) Hegel (read by) Malabou," Preface, trans. Joseph D. Cohen, in C. Malabou, *The Future of Hegel, Plasticity, Temporality and Dialectic*, trans. Lisabeth During, London: Routledge, 2005.
3 Derrida, "Time for Farewells," p. xvi.
4 Ibid., p. xvii.
5 Ibid., p. x.
6 Martin Heidegger, *The Principle of Reason*, trans. Reginald Lilly, Bloomington: Indiana University Press, 1991, p. 60: "This 'between' [*dieses Zwischen*] . . . that in some sense we leap over in the leap, or, more correctly, that we leap through as through a flame [*wie eine* Flamme]."
7 G. W. F. Hegel, *The Phenomenology of Spirit*, trans. A. V. Miller, Oxford: Oxford University Press, 1977, p. 407.
8 G. W. F. Hegel, *Lectures on the Philosophy of History*, trans. J. Sibree, New York: Dover Publications

Inc., 1956, p. 73. Admittedly, the metaphor of the phoenix also has its insufficiencies. Hegel emphasizes the fact that it is only "oriental," without any real negativity, a sun that never stops shining. Nevertheless, for Hegel the phoenix remains a good, even if naive, example, of spiritual labor.

9 J. Derrida, *Glas*, Lincoln: University of Nebraska Press, 1986, p. 102.

10 *The Phenomenology of Spirit* closes with these words from Schiller: "From the chalice of this realm of spirits/foams forth for Him his own infinitude" (p. 493).

11 Derrida, "Différance," p. 16.

12 Hegel, *Phenomenology of Spirit*, vol. II, p. 491.

13 Derrida, "Différance," p. 25.

14 Ibid., p. 22.

15 Ibid., p. 4

16 Ibid., p. 6.

17 J. Derrida, *Dissemination*, trans. Barbara Johnson, Chicago: University of Chicago Press, 1981, p. 63.

18 Derrida, "Time for Farewells," p. xxxii.

19 Ibid., p. xxxix.

20 Ibid., p. xl.

21 I should like to mention here the mythological analysis developed by Christian Berg. "The salamander, just like the phoenix, revels in the flame of the fire. The difference between the two is that the salamander stays in the fire, its legendary

immobility, which turns it into a stony element, is a better evocation of the mission to watch and to withstand death that Hegel gives to the life of the spirit." "'Retours du phénix' in 'Du mouvement et de l'immobilité de Douve' d'Yves Bonnefoy," in C. Berg, Walter Geerts, Paul Pelckmans, and Bruno Tritsmans (eds), *Retours du mythe. Vingt études pour Maurice Delcroix*, Amsterdam: Rodopi, 1996, p. 209 (my translation). But note that the salamander is the *finitude* that resists the fire. Its immobility in the flames is in fact less a sign of power than one of elementary fragility.

22 Derrida, "Time for Farewells," p. xi.
23 Derrida introduces the motif of the "un-deconstructible" in his *Specters of Marx*, New York: Routledge, 2006.
24 Derrida, "Time for Farewells," p. xlvii.

Woman's possibility, philosophy's impossibility

1 She writes further, "Even if it is the case that the domestic sphere has experienced a certain technicization since the Second World War, I agree with Angela Davis that this process has not given rise to a radical emancipation of the (non-salaried) domestic worker. [. . .] These activities are still undertaken today in a large part by unpaid feminized bodies [. . .]. In Marx's taxonomy, the

whore, the housewife, and the maid belong to the same category of servile and unproductive work and this is not just a matter of chance." Beatriz Preciado, *Testojunkie, Sexe, drogue and biopolitique*, Paris: Grasset, 2008, pp. 261–62 (my translation).

2 B. Preciado, "Multitudes Queer: note pour une politique des anormaux," online March 2003 (available at http://multitudes.samizdat.net./ Multitudes-queer). According to Preciado, this "essentialist feminism" stretches "from Irigaray to Cixous through Kristeva, from the structuralist and/or Lacanian variations on the psychoanalytic discourse (Roudinesco, Heritier, Thery)." The idea of queer multitudes "opposes parity-based politics that are derived from a biological notion of 'woman' or 'sexual difference.' It also contrasts to the universalist republican politics that concede 'recognition' and impose the 'integration' of 'differences' within the Republic. There is no sexual difference, but rather a multiplicity of differences, a transversality of power relations, a diversity of life forces."

3 Naomi Schor, "This Essentialism Which Is Not One: Coming to Grips with Irigaray," *Differences: A Journal of Feminist Cultural Studies*, No. 2, 1989, pp. 38–58. Schor writes, "What revisionism, not to say essentialism, was to Marxism-Leninism, essentialism is to feminism: the prime idiom of intellectual terrorism and the privileged

instrument of political orthodoxy. Borrowed from the time-honored vocabulary of philosophy, the word "essentialism" has been endowed within the context of feminism with the power to reduce to silence, to excommunicate, to consign to oblivion. Essentialism in modern day feminism is an anathema. There are, however, signs, encouraging signs in the form of projected books, ongoing dissertations, private conversations, not so much of a return of or to essentialism, as of a recognition of the excesses perpetrated in the name of anti-essentialism, of the urgency of rethinking the very terms of a conflict which all parties would agree has ceased to be productive" (p. 40).

Feminist Mary Russo adopts a similar approach, asserting, "The dangers of essentialism in posing the female body, whether in relation to representation or in relation to 'women's history,' have been well stated, so well stated, in fact, that 'anti-essentialism' may well be the greatest inhibition to work in cultural theory and politics at the moment and must be displaced." "Female Grotesque: Carnival and Theory," in Teresa de Lauretis (ed.), *Feminist Studies/Critical Studies*, Bloomington: Indiana University Press, 1986, p. 228.

4 Women's studies is still very underdeveloped in France, with the notable exception of the Centre d'études féminines et d'études de genre, directed

by Anne Berger at Paris-VIII University (see also above, p. 142, n. 1).

5 J. Derrida, "Women in the Beehive: A Seminar with Jacques Derrida," seminar given by Jacques Derrida in 1984 at Brown University, whose transcription is published in A. Jardine and P. Smith (eds.), *Men in Feminism*, New York: Methuen, 1987, pp. 189–203, p. 191.

6 Schor, "This Essentialism Which Is Not One," pp. 38–39.

7 Derrida, "Women in the Beehive," pp. 191–92 (my emphasis).

8 Frederic Brenner, *Diaspora: Homelands in Exile*, New York: HarperCollins, 2003. Derrida's commentary and the accompanying photograph are published in the section entitled "Voices," p. 63.

9 J. Derrida, *H.C. for Life, That Is to Say. . .*, Stanford: Stanford University Press, 2006, p. 155.

10 J. Derrida, "Choreographies," in *Points. . ., Interviews, 1974–1994*, p. 108.

11 See C. Malabou, "L'insistance de la forme. À propos du livre de Philippe Lacoue-Labarthe, *La Politique du poème*," *Poesie*, No. 105, October 2003, pp. 154–59.

12 Simone de Beauvoir, *The Second Sex*, trans. Constance Borde and Sheila Malovany-Chevallier, New York: Knopf, 2010, p. 737.

13 Ibid., p. 739.

14 Irigaray, *Ethics of Sexual Difference*, p. 107.

15 E. Levinas, "The Trace of the Other," trans. A. Lingis, in Mark C. Taylor (ed.), *Deconstruction in Context*, Chicago: University of Chicago Press, 1986, pp. 345–59, p. 358.

16 J. Derrida, *Archive Fever*, trans. Eric Prenowitz, Chicago: University of Chicago Press, 1995, p. 99.

17 Marcel Proust, "Sur le style de Flaubert," in *Écrits sur l'art*, Paris: Garnier-Flammarion, republished 1999, p. 323 (my translation).

18 Derrida, "A Time for Farewells. . ."

19 Irigaray, *Ethics of Sexual Difference*, pp. 10–11.

20 Irigaray, *This Sex Which Is Not One*, trans. Catherine Porter, Ithaca: Cornell University Press, 1985, p. 76.

21 This "vessel" has a plastic power of course, but it is entirely *mucous, obscure*, and the form it grants is not durable, the form that the female sex organ gives to the male sex organ: "In the female realm there would be the sexual act. She gives form to the male sex (organ) and sculpts it from within" (Irigaray, *Ethics of Sexual Difference*, p. 43).

22 L. Irigaray, "Une mère de glace" [An ice mother], in *Speculum of the Other Woman*, trans. Gillian C. Gill, Ithaca: Cornell University Press, 1985.

23 Butler, *Bodies That Matter*, p. 45.

24 Butler, *Gender Trouble*, p. 123.

25 Butler, *Bodies That Matter*, p. 61.

26 Irigaray, *This Sex Which Is Not One*, p. 137.

---

27 L. Irigaray, *Elementary Passions*, trans. Joanne Collie and Judith Still, New York: Routledge, 1992, p. 23.
28 Schor, "This Essentialism Which Is Not One," p. 50.
29 L. Irigaray, *Le Corps-à-corps avec la mère*, Montreal: Pleine Lune, p. 81 (my translation).
30 Irigaray, *Ethics of Sexual Difference*, p. 87.
31 Ibid., p. 88.
32 Ibid., p. 90.
33 J. Butler, *The Psychic Life of Power: Theories in Subjection*, Stanford: Stanford University Press, 1997, p. 69.
34 J. Butler, *Gender Trouble: Tenth Anniversary Edition*, New York: Routledge, 1999, p. ix.
35 Butler, *Gender Trouble*, p. 138 (my emphasis in the last sentence).
36 "The German language has preserved essence in the past participle [*gewesen*] of the verb *to be*; for essence is past – but timelessly past – being" (G. W. F. Hegel, "The Doctrine of Essence," *Science of Logic*, trans. A. V. Miller, Atlantic Highlands, NJ: American Humanities Press, 1989, p. 389).
37 Preciado, "Multitudes Queer."

Index

Index

deconstruction, 2, 7, 66, 115–16,
   118–19
   de-essentialization of woman, 96
   emancipatory transcendence,
      110
   essentialism, 97, 98
   Hegel, 71, 72, 73
   metaphysics, 106–7
   philosophy, 102
   plasticity, 63, 64–5, 120
   recovery, 72–3
   resistance to, 4
   "the un-deconstructible", 87–8
   of writing, 43
Deleuze, Gilles, 68, 143n12
deneutralization, 8–9, 33
Derrida, Jacques
   author's relationship with, 3
   deneutralization of Being, 8–9
   différance, 66, 76–7, 79
   essence, 97–8
   feminist speech, 107–9
   grammatology, 41–3, 45–7, 54
   graphic traces, 59–60
   Hanold and Gradiva, 116–17
   on Hegel, 71–2
   hetero-affection, 20–1
   inviolability, 34–5
   on Irigaray, 15–16
   on Levinas, 21–2, 26
   the mouth, 19
   ontic-ontological imperialism of
      the feminine, 30
   ontological difference, 6, 36
   philosophical invention, 67–71
   phoenix paradigm, 74
   plasticity, 79–80, 119–20
   recovery, 67, 78
   semiology, 43–4, 148n8
   sexual difference, 32–3
   Stimmung, 30–1
   sublation, 88

supplements, 83
   "the un-deconstructible", 87–8
   women rabbis, 105–6
   women's studies, 103
   wonder, 146n43
   writing, 47–54, 56–7, 65
Descartes, René, 10–11, 13, 16–17,
   31, 143n10, 143n12, 146n43
différance, 3, 55, 66, 76–7, 79, 81
   deconstruction, 72
   plasticity, 62–3, 87
   repression of form, 65
   supplements, 83
difference, 3, 35–6, 66
   change of, 121
   deneutralization of, 31
   plasticity, 36, 64–5
   wonder as passion of, 11,
      143n10, 143n12
   writing and, 50, 55
   see also gender difference;
      ontological difference; sexual
      difference
discrimination, 92
domestic violence, 90–1, 94, 96
domestic work, 94, 153n1
domesticity, 24
domination, 1, 95
dual exploitation, 93–4
Duras, Marguerite, 102

essence, 2, 95, 96–9, 122, 125–6,
   139
   accident and, 88, 89
   arche-writing, 50
   biological, 138
   domesticity, 24
   fugitive, 100, 140
   Hegel on, 136, 158n36
   Heidegger on, 8, 136
   meaning of the feminine, 29,
      39

160

Index

Index

Index

412011

Index

stem cells, 80–1, 84, 85–6
Stimmung, 30–1, 150n26
sublation, 71, 74, 79, 87, 88
substitutability, 37, 38, 56
supplementarity, 54, 55, 83, 86, 87
synaptic traces, 58–9, 62

Talmud, 25–6
texts, 54, 77–8, 131–2
the trace, 58–60, 116, 120–1
  différance, 76–7
  erasure of, 78
  graphic traces, 59–60, 62, 65, 66
  plasticity, 62–3, 121–2
  spider paradigm, 75–6
trans-differentiation, 80–1, 84, 85
transgender, 14, 133
transvestitism, 37, 38, 133–5

"the un-deconstructible", 87–8

vagina, 5
  see also vulva
violence, 90–1, 99, 122
  acts by women, 23–4
  anti-essentialist, 96, 109, 139
  concept of woman, 93–4
  to the other, 30
  philosophical, 100, 101, 110,
    141

resistance to, 2
specificity, 98
vulva, 5, 16, 18–19, 29

wage inequality, 91–2
woman
  body of, 14–15
  concept of, 8, 10, 92–3, 135–6
  essentialism, 94–5, 96–9
  the feminine as distinct from, 24,
    36
  Irigaray on, 131
  Levinas on, 21, 23, 26
  materiality of, 125, 130
  non-place of, 122–3, 139
  reduction of the feminine to, 21
  see also the feminine
women philosophers, 3, 99–102,
    106–14, 118–19, 122, 131,
    140–1
women's studies, 5, 103–4, 155n4
  see also gender studies
wonder, 10–13, 27–8, 30, 31,
    143n10, 143n12, 146n43
work, 91–2, 94
wounds, 73, 75, 80
writing, 41–2, 46, 47–57, 120–1
  assimilated to woman, 116
  plasticity, 43, 63–5
  "psychic", 60–1

164